THE FRONTIER SEA

The Napoleonic Wars in the Adriatic

DAVE WATSON

Copyright © Dave Watson 2023

The right of Dave Watson to be identified as the author of this book has been asserted by him in accordance with the Copyright, Design and Patents Act of 1988.

All rights reserved. No part of this publication may be reproduced, stored in a retrieval system, or transmitted, in any form, or by any means, electronic, mechanical, photocopying, recording or otherwise, without the express written consent of the author.

Every reasonable effort has been made to trace copyright holders and to obtain their permission for the use of copyright material. The author and publisher apologise for any errors or omissions in this work, and would be grateful if notified of any corrections that should be incorporated in future reprints or editions of this book.

Balkan Military History
www.balkanhistory.org

Cover designed by Henry Hyde. Printing is the French frigate *Pomone* fighting HMS *Alceste* and HMS *Active* during the Action of 29 November 1811. Painted by Pierre-Julien Gilbert.

ISBN: 978-1-80443-036-1 (paperback)
ISBN: 978-1-80443-037-8 (ebook)

Most of the great powers contested the lands around the Adriatic Sea during the Napoleonic Wars. While never a major theatre of operations, the Adriatic was part of the overall strategy of most of the combatants. It played an essential role by influencing alliances and diverting troops and ships, which all contributed to the defeat of Napoleon. The Napoleonic Wars was also a period of significant change, with the French and British intervening in a region that had long been a battleground reserved for the Austrian, Russian and Ottoman empires.

This book examines the Adriatic campaigns, including those rarely mentioned in the history of the period, and the armies, navies and personalities that fought in the region between 1797 and 1815. Austrian, French, Russian, British, and their foreign regiments fought up and down the coast, sometimes with or against local leaders like Peter I of Montenegro and Ali Pasha of Ioannina. Many commanders were far from home, with orders taking weeks to reach them. This meant even junior officers could take military and diplomatic decisions usually reserved for more senior officers.

This is a story of strategy and small wars with many colourful personalities playing their part in a fascinating, if violent, tale against the backdrop of the frontier sea.

CONTENTS

Prologue vii
Introduction xi

Chapter 1:   The Adriatic before 1797 1
             Russia 2
             Ottoman Empire 3
             Austria 5
             Venice 6
             Naval Warfare 8

Chapter 2:   War comes to the Adriatic—1797-1802 11
             Ionian Islands 14
             The Russians enter the Mediterranean 18
             Ali Pasha and the French 22
             The War of Second Coalition 1799-1801 23

Chapter 3:   Small Wars in the Balkans 27
             The Military Border 27
             The Ottoman Frontier 31
             Border conflicts 38
             Ali Pasha 43

Chapter 4:   French Expansion—1802-09 51
             Italy 54
             Dalmatian Campaign of 1806 56

	Naval attack on Istanbul	65
	Russo-Turkish War 1806-09	67
	1st Serbian Revolt	72
	Adriatic manoeuvres	75
Chapter 5:	France on the Defensive 1810-15	81
	Russo-Turkish War 1809-12	81
	British Adriatic Offensive	82
	Kingdom of Naples	99
	Serbian revolt reignites	101
Chapter 6:	Armed Forces in the Adriatic	103
	France	103
	Russia	111
	Britain	114
	Ottoman Empire	121
	Montenegro	127
	Austria	129
Chapter 7:	Conclusion	131
Appendix 1:	Chronology	133
Appendix 2:	Wargaming the Adriatic Conflicts	137
Notes		149
Bibliography		151
Acknowledgments		157
Endnotes		159
About the Author		167

PROLOGUE

Life in the Royal Navy could be brutal. Lieutenant Donat Henchy O'Brien viewed the gun deck of the frigate HMS *Amphion* after the Battle of Lissa in 1811: 'It would be difficult to describe the horrors which now presented themselves. The carnage was dreadful—the dead and dying lying about in every direction; the cries of the latter were most lamentable and piercing.'[1]

A double-shotted cannonball fired from an 18-pounder gun could do terrible damage. As O'Brien explained, 'Strange to say, every man stationed at one of the guns had been killed, and as it was supposed by the same shots, which passed through both sides of the ship into the sea. At another gun the skull of one poor creature was lodged in the beam above where he stood, the shot having taken an oblique direction: in short, the scene was heart-rending and sickening.' If the actual fighting was not bad enough, sailors in the Adriatic also faced a wind called the *bora*. A Russian naval officer, Midshipman Vladimir Bronevskiy in his history of the campaign, said, 'It was so strong that it can be compared to a terrible hurricane.'[2] His frigate rolled on its side, masts cracked, and scraps of torn sail flew by.

Life was pretty challenging on land as well, particularly if you were a French soldier struggling down the tracks that passed for roads in Dalmatia, with the threat of ambush around every corner. There was no prison camp for those captured by the Montenegrins, who cut off the heads of enemies who fell into their hands. They were no less ruthless with their own and allied wounded. An older, somewhat overweight Russian officer fell from exhaustion during a retreat from a raid. A Montenegrin rushed to him and drew his sword, saying, 'you're very brave and must wish that I take your head. Say a prayer and cross yourself.'³ Unsurprisingly, the Russian gathered his strength and caught up! If this sounds grim, you certainly would not want to get on the wrong side of the Ottoman governor Ali Pasha. Every French soldier captured by him at the Greek port of Preveza was given a razor with which he was forced to skin the severed heads of his compatriots.

Garrison duty should have been a rest, with the attractions of cheap wine and friendly local women. However, Lieutenant John Hildebrand of the 35th Foot described one barracks as having 'a large admixture of fleas of the largest size and in high condition.' Soldiers stripped naked to get rid of them from their uniforms, shaking out 'large lumps of fleas, in balls formed by their tenacious clinging to each other and one would fancy almost devouring each other, a truly wonderful and disgusting sight! So strange as hardly to be believed excepting by those who beheld it.'⁴

However, there were some compensations. The weather was generally pleasant when the *bora* or the *mistral* winds did not blow. It could also be profitable for naval officers and crews who acquired prize money from the many ships they captured. The local merchants and ship owners were less enthusiastic about the impact on the local economy! Captain William Hoste wrote home to his father, 'We have plenty of work cut out for us in the Adriatic, and of all stations it is the pleasantest: such variety and amusement, and prizes to boot, make the hours pass quick, I assure you.'⁵

In our story, we will meet these characters and many others: the French, Italian, British, Austrian, Russian, Ottoman and local soldiers and sailors who plied their trade in the Adriatic during the Napoleonic Wars.

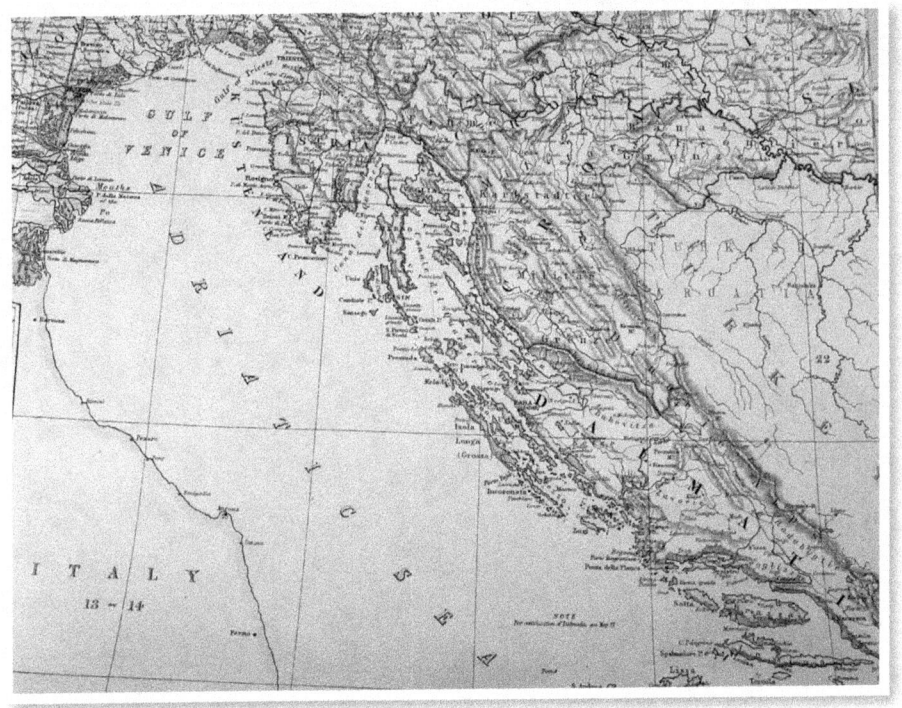

The Adriatic Sea. From the map *Austrian Empire* by
W. Johnson in 1875 (Author's collection).

INTRODUCTION

The Adriatic Sea is thought to be named after the Etruscan colony of Adria, founded in 1376 BCE, once the most important town in the Adriatic but now in ruins. The Adriatic is about 460 miles long and generally between 90 and 110 miles wide, although only 37 miles wide at its narrowest point. The area covered by the Adriatic is around forty thousand square miles. The Italian coast to its west is generally low-lying and navigable, with few major ports. In contrast, the eastern shore has high mountains and deep water, bordered by islands and rocks, which make navigation challenging.

The focus of this story is the region on the eastern shore of the Adriatic Sea from Istria (in modern Croatia) in the north to Albania and Greece in the south. The coastline is mainly a narrow belt of land dominated by the Dinaric Alps, which helped create a hinterland utterly different from the more urbanised and prosperous coast. Seventy-nine islands run almost parallel to the coast, the largest being Brač, Pag, Hvar, and further south, Corfu. Because of their position on the coastal shipping lanes which joined the western and eastern worlds, the Adriatic islands have often played an important historical role. The coastal cities were not large during this period. They included Trieste in the north, Rijeka, Zadar, Split, Ragusa (Dubrovnik), Cattaro (Kotor), and Ioannina in the south.

However, the Adriatic conflict did not occur in isolation. The Ottomans had broader concerns in the Balkans, not the least of which were perennial war with the Russians and internal disputes. The British campaign was directed mainly from Sicily, meaning that events in Naples and later Spain often dominated its plans. For the French, Russians, and Austrians, the campaigns in central Europe were decisive. The Austrian and Ottoman empires faced each other on the coast and inland in a border area that, by our period, became known as Krajina.

Much has been written about the land borders in the Balkans, the scene of violent conflicts for centuries. However, the Adriatic Sea itself was a key extension of those borderlands, which the sociologist Emilio Cocco called the 'maritime counterpart to the [Balkan] space poised between East and West'.[6] A frontier that was contested fiercely by the Venetian and Ottoman empires just before our period became even more fluid as the French, British and Russians entered the Adriatic. It is a porous boundary that is difficult to capture in a line on a map, but still a marker of identity for those who lived beside it—a frontier of the sea.

Our story begins with the French Revolutionary Wars that brought French armies into the Adriatic region due to their victories in Italy. Historians differ over when the Revolutionary Wars ended and the Napoleonic Wars started, but either way, Napoleon Bonaparte led the French forces in our area throughout the period. Napoleon captured Venice on 12 May 1797 during the War of the First Coalition. While Austria gained Venice under the Treaty of Campo Formio (12 October 1797), the Ionian Islands off the Greek coast were ceded to France.

As our story continues, we will cover the subsequent conflicts that resulted in control of the territories shifting amongst the great powers of the day. In addition to the interventions of France and Austria, the Ottoman Empire held Bosnia and, on paper, Montenegro, Albania and Greece. However, in practice, the Montenegrins acted independently, as did another key character in our story: Ali Pasha, who controlled much of Albania and northwest Greece.

Other powers also intervened in the region. The Russians captured the Ionian Islands in 1799, although they surrendered them in 1807. They also engaged in one of many wars against the Ottomans that in the 19th century were less about capturing 'Russian' lands and more about the Slavic peoples of the Balkans and control of the Straits between Asia and Europe. The British dominated the Adriatic Sea from bases in the Ionian Islands and on the island of Lissa (Vis) in 1812. Our story ends in 1814, when the French abandoned the Ionian Islands.

This theatre of operations is geographically detached from the main battlefields of the Napoleonic Wars, although it was active throughout the conflict and impacted the overall war effort of the participants. In his history of the

Napoleonic Wars[7], David Gates described it as 'minestrone soup', meaning all the great powers had an interest and dabbled in it.

Communications in the Napoleonic era were slow, with a message taking weeks to reach the commander on the spot. This meant commanders in the Adriatic region had much more freedom of operation than did their colleagues elsewhere. This was true for all the nations involved. Paris to Ragusa (Dubrovnik) is a journey of almost two thousand kilometres along roads that at the time were often little more than dirt tracks. From Moscow, the same destination is nearly three thousand kilometres. Students of Wellington will know he strongly discouraged independent action, in fairness, not least because he had command of Britain's only significant army. But this level of control was not possible in the Adriatic, 2,200km from London and nearly 900km (including a sea journey) from the theatre commander based in Sicily. We will hear from the memoirs of John Hildebrand (35th Foot) how even a lowly subaltern was given an independent command. Naval commanders were more used to individual initiative. Still, even they could find themselves having to take military and sometimes diplomatic decisions that would usually be reserved for more senior officers.

British naval power was crucial to achieving strategic objectives in the Adriatic and the wider Mediterranean, but it was not decisive. As Palmerston put it, 'Ships sailing on the sea cannot stop armies on land.' However, the Royal Navy did achieve this in a limited way in the Adriatic. British subsidies, funded by trade and economic strength, were a critical factor influencing warfare on land. A historical tradition connects British policy in the region to a fear of Napoleon invading India. While Napoleon may have had such a dream, it was not realistic, even when allied to Tsar Paul of Russia.

Napoleon only visited the northern tip of the Adriatic himself[8], but he saw himself in historical terms. Writing later in St Helena, he recalled, 'Greece awaits a liberator. What a splendid wreath of glory is there! He can inscribe his name for eternity with those of Homer, of Plato, of Epaminondas! When at the time of campaign of Italy I touched the shores of the Adriatic, I wrote to the Directoire that I could look out over the Empire of Alexander.'[9]

British policy was focused more on the Ottoman Empire, whose collapse would have allowed France to grab the spoils. French progress down the Dalmatian coast, mainly at Austrian expense, reduced the buffer between the French and Ottoman empires. Austria was Britain's leading ally during these wars, and British subsidies kept them in the conflict. They were France's most consistent enemy, joining all bar one of the coalitions formed to fight them. The Ottoman Empire is traditionally viewed as being in decline since the reign of Süleyman the Great. In fact, the empire's boundaries shifted very little in the century after his death. However, much was going on within those borders. As Caroline Finkel explains, border maps are 'masking the reality that any frontier, however defined, was a place of infinite complication both for the governments that sought to assert their power there, or acknowledged it as the limit of their reach, and for the people whose lives were shaped by its very existence.'[10] Borderlands are often far from the seat of power and, as we will see, create challenges for the states trying to control them. Diverse populations can learn to live with each other while also perceiving others as different and hostile, leading to violence. In the Balkans, these borders were disputed, becoming the scene for wars between the great powers.

There is much debate amongst historians as to how different warfare was in the Napoleonic Wars compared with that in the 18th century. The armies were indeed larger, sustained by revolutionary France by extracting resources from conquered territories and reorganisation of French society. The revolution created an officer class dominated by talent rather than birth. However, the loss of experienced officers had a large impact on the fleet, which was crucial in the Adriatic. As Jeremy Black argues, the army's tactical changes represented a continuation of tendencies already adopted, such as rapid movement and battlefield artillery; the crucial difference was numbers.[11] Napoleon may have inherited these changes, but he did bring self-confidence, swift decision-making, mobility, and the concentration of forces.

Historians also differ over the blame for the wars that caused much suffering in this region, as they did in the rest of Europe. Charles Esdaile argues that the responsibility was Napoleon's 'and his alone.' While accepting that Napoleon played a major role in provoking the wars, David Gates argues, 'He assuredly did not start them all.' He points in particular to Austria's conduct, but the other belligerents also played their part. Charles Esdaile does have a point when he argues that the impact of revolutionary ideology was somewhat blunted in Italy and the Balkans by the looting and depredations of the French army. Revolts and desertion rates amongst locally-raised troops were exceptionally high. However, the conflict had longer-term consequences, influencing the nationalist movements later in the century. The *ancien* regimes paid the price for failing to address these developments at the Congress of Vienna at the conclusion of the Napoleonic Wars. For the Ottomans, acquiring new weaponry was not enough; the failure to reform the civil and military structures underpinned their failures.

As the great Napoleonic historian David Chandler said, 'I have never underestimated the value of wargaming as an aid to serious study as well as a means of relaxation.'[12] As he recognised, it is no surprise that the Napoleonic Wars are popular with wargamers. The battles of the coalitions against Napoleon, the Peninsular War, and finally, Waterloo are regularly fought on the tabletop. However, the campaigns in the Adriatic offer something different, both in scale and variety. We will explore these options and offer some scenarios in Appendix 2.

Place names in the Balkans are a perennial challenge for the writer and reader. I have generally used place names as they were described during this period, although with alternatives and modern names in parentheses. The Ottomans create a further complexity; I generally refer to the Ottoman Empire rather than the everyday use of Turkey or today, Türkiye. 'The Porte' is used as a shorthand for the Sublime Porte when referring to actions of the Ottoman administration and diplomatic exchanges. I prefer Istanbul to Constantinople to reflect the Ottoman control of the city and the gradual shift in name. However, it can be argued that this did not formally change until the Turkish Post Office officially changed the name in 1930. The Ottomans and other South Slavs also called the Mediterranean, or the Aegean, the White Sea, creating further confusion.

Dates can also confuse as some countries still used the Julian calendar in this period. I generally refer to the modern calendar. There are some chronological overlaps in the narrative because it was better to finish a particular campaign. A single narrative would not accommodate the complex interventions by local and external actors or capture some of the distinct features of warfare in this region. There is a chronology in Appendix 1 to give the reader an overview.

CHAPTER ONE

THE ADRIATIC BEFORE 1797

For most of the 18th century, the Balkans had settled borders, on paper at least. The Habsburg Empire faced the Ottoman Empire along a border primarily defined by the Treaty of Karlowitz in 1699, following Prince Eugene's destruction of the Ottoman army at the Battle of Zenta in 1697. The border separated Croatia and Slavonia (not to be confused with modern Slovenia) from Ottoman Bosnia and Serbia. The exception was Dalmatia, mostly a possession of Venice, which, along with the Ionian Islands, connected the ports that had been part of the Venetian trading empire for several centuries. Also on the Dalmatian coast was the Republic of Ragusa (Dubrovnik), which maintained its independence while paying tribute to the Ottomans. It was a useful entrepot for the Ottomans, a bit like Hong Kong for China. Eugene's return to the Balkans in 1716 made further inroads into Ottoman territory, including Belgrade[1]. However, the Ottomans recovered these lands in a successful campaign that began in 1736[2]. What would later become known as the 'sick man of Europe' still had a kick in him!

Russia

The Ottomans fared less well in the eastern Balkans, where the Russians made inroads during the Russo-Turkish War of 1768–74, weakening Ottoman control of Wallachia and Moldavia. This was followed by a further war (1787-92), with Russia and Austria combining to push the Ottomans out of Wallachia, Moldavia and much of Bosnia and Serbia. However, pressure from other European powers following the French Revolution forced the Austrians to abandon their conquests. Russia was left with modest gains.

The Ottomans broadly welcomed the revolution because it gave them six years of peace, and they generally avoided aligning with either side. The death of Catherine the Great in 1796 brought some respite from Russian aggression as Tsar Paul sought a rapprochement with the Ottomans and access for his ships through the Straits into the Adriatic and the eastern Mediterranean. Russia's expanding borders in Ukraine and later in the Balkans brought agricultural advances and revenue, although these were constrained by the need for military expenditures to protect them. As McNeill puts it, 'The truly enormous achievement of Russia's nobility and bureaucracy in superintending the process and taxing the result made Russia between 1762 and 1815 the arbiter of eastern Europe and allowed Russian might to outstrip Austrian and eclipse Ottoman power.'[3]

The Russians were increasingly drawn into the Balkans by two issues: Ottoman policies towards the Slavic peoples, and control of the Straits. However, unlike his later successors, Tsar Alexander (23 March 1801–19 November 1825) was never willing to risk a European war for Russia's Slavic brothers. There was also long-standing internal opposition from many in the nobility to this expansionist foreign policy[4]. Control of the Straits brought the risk of a war with the British and the complete collapse of the Ottoman state, which could bring more powerful enemies to the Russian border[5]. Instead, Russian policy was to force the Ottomans to recognise Russia as the protector of the Christian population in their empire and to regulate access through the Straits.

The castle of Rumeli Hisar defended the Straits
from the Black Sea entrance (Author)

Ottoman Empire

The idea that the sultan simply had to command and it was done, if ever valid, had almost entirely gone by this period. The effects of military losses were to exacerbate the decentralisation of the empire that had developed throughout the 18th century with the partial breakdown of Ottoman central authority and with the development of semi-independent rulers (*ayans*). While this process accelerated later in the century, recent research indicates there was considerable interdependence between the *ayans* and the Ottoman central government (Sublime Porte) during this period. The Ottomans had to fight on multiple fronts, which increased their reliance on local forces. In the Balkans they faced the Austrians on the Danube and the Russians around the Black Sea.

By the late 18th century, there were ten *ayans* in the Balkans, the strongest of which were Pasvanoglu Osman Pasha, based in Vidin, and Tependenli Ali Pasha. Albania was divided into three pashaliks: Scutari, Berat, and Ioannina. Ali was based in Ioannina and controlled much of mainland Greece and southern Albania. He was probably born around 1750 (sources differ). He led an armed band that challenged Ottoman officials in Albania and Epirus, although he came from a family of pashas. Like other such leaders, he was co-opted into the administrative-military apparatus of the Ottoman Empire, holding various posts until 1788, when he was appointed pasha, ruler of the sanjak of Ioannina. Both *ayans* dealt directly with other powers, and Ali Pasha played an important role in the Adriatic campaigns. The Porte relied heavily on the *ayans* for their armies during the wars against Russia and Austria, making it difficult to reassert control after the conflicts.

Ali Pasha (Author's collection)

The general decline in Ottoman institutions speeded up in the late 18th century with administrative posts sold to the highest bidder. This included the right to collect taxes, allowing tax farmers to collect what they wanted, keeping ever larger portions for themselves and extorting more tax. The system increased dissatisfaction with the state, 'The people no longer knew their way in or out... which tyrant to pay first'[6]. These local elites were not exclusively Muslims. Christian notables were called *kocabasi* or *corbaci*, and also extorted the peasants and enriched themselves at the cost of the state. Bruno Mungai concludes, 'The Ottoman state's financial ability to make wars profitable and desirable enterprises was compromised.'[7]

Ottoman rule in Montenegro had always been weak, and Prince-Bishop Peter I Niegos Petrovich, who became the ruling prince in 1782, was able to develop his autonomy further during this period. He visited Russia in 1778 and 1785 to seek support, with limited success, as elements in the Russian court favoured Ali Pasha. On his return in 1785, he faced an invasion by the forces of the pasha of Scutari, which he resisted. In 1796 a second invasion by the pasha of Scutari led to a series of Montenegrin victories. The pasha was captured and beheaded, and by a treaty in 1799 the Ottomans recognised the independence of Montenegro.

Sultan Mehmet III and his Grand Vizer, Halil Hamit, supported traditional reforms, improving the weapons and discipline of the older corps while introducing new technology into the artillery and the navy. The new 'had to be isolated from the old so that the equilibrium of Ottoman society would not be upset.'[8] His son, Sultan Selim III (1789-1807), succeeded him in April 1789. He was well-educated, fond of literature and calligraphy, and wrote many poems. He spoke Arabic, Persian, Turkish and Old Bulgarian fluently. He had engaged with foreigners and their ideas, and agreed with his father on the need to reform the state. The military defeats by the Russians and Austrians enabled him to begin military reforms, which included new barracks, regular pay, and weeding out inactive soldiers, halving the Janissary rolls. These reforms made limited progress in the older corps but were more successful in the artillery. Selim went further in 1794, creating a new infantry corps, the *Nizam-I Cedit*, organised on western lines. The navy was also reorganised with French assistance, including modern ships and a naval school to train officers. However, civil reforms were piecemeal, and failed to ensure that the state's finances could adequately fund military reform. As a result, the Empire was in decline after the mid-18th century, postponing disaster by emergency measures and working with European powers to preserve their independence.

Austria

The Habsburgs organised their new lands in the Balkans into two political units, Civil Croatia and Civil Slavonia. Civil Croatia was headed by the Ban (governor), appointed by the crown and usually a Hungarian, advised by a Diet (parliament) of the nobility, which also sent representatives to the Hungarian Diet. By the outset of the Napoleonic Wars, Habsburg reforms had centralised power away from Civil Croatia, and attempts to make German the language of administration were particularly resented. Civil Slavonia had even less autonomy, and the region was repopulated by German and Hungarian landowners. Few of the political conflicts had changed the lot of the peasants who lived under feudal conditions. The emancipation of the serfs in 1785 resulted in some modest improvements, such as limiting payments to thirty per cent of their income.

Between the civil regions and the Ottomans was the Military Border (Militargrenze), under the direct control of the emperor. It was initially populated by refugees from Serbia and Bosnia, who were granted plots of land in return for military service. These soldiers were not serfs, and lived in self-administering communities based on zadrugas (household communities). This arrangement was resented by the nobles in Civil Croatia and Slavonia and the Catholic church, which all opposed the special status it gave to the Serbian Orthodox population.

Regimental reforms in the second half of the 18th century improved military discipline, and troops could be called upon to fight elsewhere. A small war continued with the Ottomans across the border, in addition to their duties of maintaining fortifications and keeping a strict quarantine along the Military Border.

Venice

Venice, for so long a dominant player in the Adriatic, was in terminal decline. Through many of the great conflicts of the 18th century, Venice maintained a determined neutrality. While this served her economically, it also encouraged the neglect of her once all-powerful fleet. After the replacement of the oared galley by the sailing ship, Venice relied on foreign-built ships, leaving her shipbuilding industry hopelessly outdated. Foreign ships operated in the Adriatic without challenge, and the Habsburgs, by making Trieste a free port, forced the Venetians to end their old protectionist policy. Humiliatingly, Venice was even forced to pay an annual bribe to the Barbary Coast pirates to sail through seas they used to command. Some ground was recovered in the 1786 naval campaign; still, in 1794 only 309 Venetian merchant ships were listed on the state register.

The French Revolution may have sent shock waves throughout Europe, but in Venice, the response to requests to join military alliances was just the same: Neutrality has served us well; we can look after ourselves. However, long before the French armies appeared in Italy, Venice was being undermined from within. Peace and the pursuit of pleasure created a culture that rejected even armed neutrality, with fewer than five thousand ill-equipped troops scattered in small garrisons. The French complained that Venice had harboured the Comte de Lille, the brother of the dead King Louis, and Venice allowed Austrian troops to cross their territory. When Napoleon Bonaparte defeated the Austrians in 1796, Venice again allowed Austrian troops to retreat through their territory and even occupy the admittedly crumbling fortress at Peschiera.

Napoleon threatened to burn Verona if the Venetians did not hand over key bridges and supply his troops—a bluff the Venetians fell for, as Napoleon reported to the Directory, 'I have purposely engineered this quarrel, in case you wish to get five or six millions out of Venice.'[9]

The Arsenale in Venice where fleets were built (Author).

All too late, the Senate ordered the fleet back to the Lagoon, to hear that only four obsolete galleys and seven galliots were even partially ready for service. Although Anderson[10] lists eight ships of the line, six frigates, and eleven galleys based in Corfu, and identifies thirteen ships of the line on the stocks in Venice, along with seven frigates. A decision to rebuild the army was halted when France objected that the Senate had not taken such an action when the Austrians breached Venice's borders.

Napoleon then offered an alliance, which was refused, probably because the whole concept of revolutionary France was an anathema to the wealthy families controlling the Senate. Their views were increasingly not supported by the Republic's citizens. French-inspired revolts in the *terra firma* led to Venice arming a militia that opened fire on French troops foraging and looting villages. This led to an ultimatum, delivered by Napoleon's *aide-de-camp* General Junot. A cringing apology was undermined by a further insurrection in Verona against the French garrison, and the sinking of a French naval ship approaching the Lagoon.

Without consultation, Napoleon and the Austrians signed the Peace of Leoben (18 April 1797), which handed over Venice's Istrian and Dalmatian ports to Austria with much of the *terra firma*. Napoleon's final ultimatum demanded an end to the Republic, and its replacement by a French-appointed Provisional Municipality supported by a French garrison. On Friday, 12 May 1797, the Venetian Great Council voted to accept it—and the Venetian Republic was no more. In the final peace treaty with Austria (Treaty of Campo Formio) on 17 October, Napoleon handed over the city to Austria while destroying all the ships that he could not remove.

Naval Warfare

Successful campaigns in the Adriatic almost always required control of the sea. To understand the naval war, we need to start with the challenges that sailing in the Adriatic brought to the sailors of the period. The Dalmatian coast was dominated by islands, rocks and sandbanks off the mouths of rivers. This made navigation challenging, and maps were not of the standard they are today. The memoirs of sailors serving in the Adriatic refer to inaccurate maps and even inexperienced pilots.

Then there were the winds. A meteorological journal kept in Venice for five years[11] recorded that at the head of the Adriatic, southerly winds are most frequent during the summer months to September. The wind is seldom from the northward between April and July, and is generally variable during fifteen days of each month in the year. The *bora* is a northerly to northeasterly katabatic or drainage wind that carries high-density air from a higher elevation down a slope under the force of gravity in areas near the Adriatic Sea. The strongest bora winds occur near the Velebit mountain range along the coast of Dalmatia and can reach hurricane speeds of 220km/h. They blow strongest and for longer in the winter months.

The Russian naval officer Bronevskiy described his first contact, 'The wind, with an apparent aspiration and an extraordinary strength, burst from behind the mountains, raising clouds of dust, tearing out trees and peeling the roofs of houses.' Ships were often dismasted, and sailors kept a weather eye for the telltale signs which could arrive before they had time to furl the sails. Even ports were not safe havens. For example, ships avoided Fiume in winter and sheltered in Buccari (Bakar), 9km away. In December 1811, the French frigate *Flora* (44) was surprised by a bora on her passage from Trieste to Venice, which threw her onto the coast near Chioggia, losing the ship and two-thirds of the crew.

Another strong wind, the *sirocco*, can blow from the south at speeds up to 100km/hr, carrying red dust from North Africa. In the winter, it brings densely foggy weather. The Russians from the Baltic fleet found this particularly tough and reported that the pitch of their ships melted and the cannons were too hot to touch. Bronevskiy described its breeze as 'similar to the noise of a flame emanating from a closed vent.' Other winds, including the *mistral*, created their own challenges depending on the season.

There were surprisingly detailed guides to the currents and weather in the Adriatic. For example, Vincenzo di Luccio's 1798 guide was translated into English and published in London in 1806[12]. It describes the currents and the weather a mariner might expect in each section of the Adriatic coast down to Albania in each season, as well as sandbanks and anchorages. It must have been the bible for French and Royal Navy officers sailing in these waters.

Some trade in the Adriatic was carried out by conventional two- and three-masted ships, but the main carrier was the *trabàccolo*, a small seagoing ship of between fifty and seventy tons with two lugsails and a jib. These carried every sort of cargo between the Adriatic ports, and being small, they could take refuge in the little fortified harbours that dotted the coast, or hide in bays when a predatory warship was sighted. When captured, they rarely put up a fight, and their cargos were seized as prizes. However, some were armed with two or three cannon. On 18 February 1801, off the island of Lafrina, the cutter HMS *Pigmy* (14) captured *Adelaide*, a French privateer trabàccolo armed with two 12-pounders and one 6-pounder cannon, and carrying a crew of fifty-one men.

Trabàccolo (Akerbeltz, CC BY-SA 4.0)

This was a profitable activity for the navies operating in the Adriatic, but ruinous to the local economy. It was also the subject of extensive litigation in British courts (Lords Commissioners of Appeals in Prize Causes), which for this region was in Malta. You can read these very detailed appeals today in the National Archives, which give a good picture of trade in the Mediterranean and the complexity of ownership, cargos, the documentation needed, and the rules surrounding the blockade of enemy ports.[13] This reminds us that naval warfare was an extension of economic warfare. By 1811 there were 803 vessels based in Malta, five times more than in 1803, with a naval squadron to protect smuggling interests.

CHAPTER TWO

WAR COMES TO THE ADRIATIC—1797-1802

The Treaty of Campo Formio ended Austrian involvement in the First Coalition and provided the starting point for the conflict in the Adriatic. The youthful Napoleon Bonaparte (twenty-six years old) had taken command of the disgruntled Army of Italy in Nice on 27 March 1796, saying, 'I will lead you into the most fertile plains on earth. Rich provinces, opulent towns, all shall be at your disposal; there you will find honour, glory and riches. Soldiers of Italy! Will you be lacking in courage or endurance?'[1] Napoleon clearly understood that adequate food and the right to loot meant more than the propaganda mission of the French Republic!

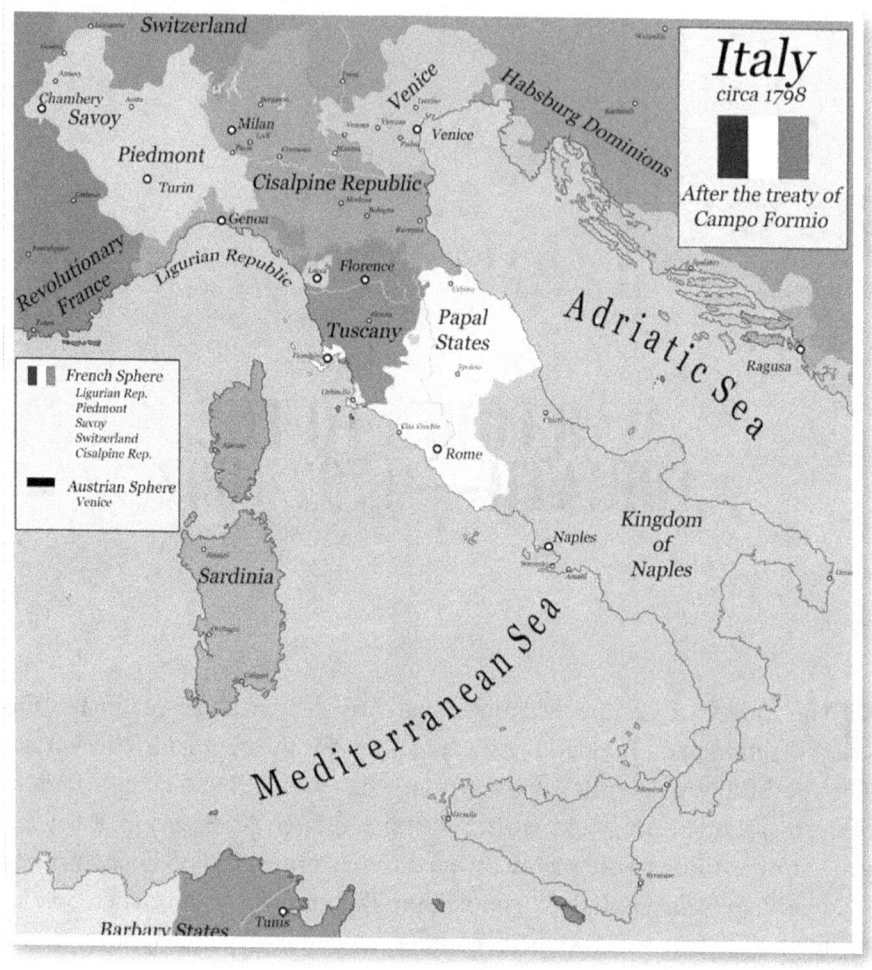

(Jcooksey1, CC BY-SA 4.0)

Italy was not the unified country it is today. Instead, it contained twelve major disunited principalities, all hostile to the French Republic, even if their citizens were becoming more sympathetic. The Army of Italy had been reduced to around thirty-seven thousand effectives, but they did not let their young general down. By 28 April, he had knocked Piedmont out of the war, and defeated a major Austrian army at the Battle of Lodi on 10 May. Reinforced to around fifty thousand men, he pinned the Austrians at Mantua and struck south, occupying Tuscany and defeating the Papal States at Fort

Urban. Then, shifting his forces northwards, he defeated the Austrian General Wurmser's much larger army at the battles of Lonato and Castiglioni. This forced the Austrians back into the Alps before a reinforced Wurmser returned to attempt the relief of Mantua. Further defeats led to Wurmser's replacement by Alvinczy, who initially drove the French back before a narrow defeat at Arcole (15-17 November 1796). After a further reorganisation, Napoleon defeated Alvinczy at Rivoli on 14 January 1797, leading to Mantua's fall. This enabled Napoleon to take his army into Austria. When he was within one hundred miles of Vienna, the Austrians sued for peace.

This was Napoleon's first experience of large-scale warfare, yet in this campaign, we can see the basis for his later success. He made mistakes and was fortunate to face average Austrian commanders with an over-rigid adherence to the military ideas of a previous era. However, despite limited resources, he maintained the tactical offensive, pursuing and attacking his generally stronger opponents without respite. He always sought to concentrate his forces on the battlefield while the Austrians frequently divided theirs, leading to defeat in detail. As David Chandler concludes, in March 1796 Napoleon was comparatively unknown, and this campaign marked the emergence of one of the greatest captains of all time. 'The young eagle had found his wings; the future lay with destiny.'[2]

The Treaty of Campo Formio brought the French to the Adriatic shores of Italy by creating the Cisalpine Republic, the Roman Republic, and the Parthenopean Republic. These republics were modeled on the French Republic, nominally autonomous but in practice directed by the French. The treaty gave the French naval bases on the Adriatic, including the Papal port of Ancona. Napoleon was keen to keep the port; hinting at future plans, he wrote to the Directoire, 'Ancona is a very good port, within 24 hours of Macedonia and ten days of Constantinople. We must keep Ancona when peace is made, and maintain it under the French flag; it will give us a hold on Turkey.'[3] This was already used as a base for French privateers who quickly brought Austrian coastal trade to a standstill. The Austrian navy had only a handful of gunboats in the Trieste squadron, so a Royal Navy squadron under Captain Tyler was dispatched to the Adriatic. However, when Spain joined France, all the ships were withdrawn, leaving the Austrians unsupported. Six French vessels, including *Brune* (22) under Captain Sibile, harassed Austrian convoys, even into Venice itself.

Ionian Islands

The treaty also stretched French rule across the Adriatic to the Ionian Islands. Traditionally called the Heptanese (Seven Islands), the group includes many smaller islands as well as the seven principal ones. Six of the larger islands, Zakynthos, Ithaca, Corfu, Kefalonia, Lefkada and Paxi (Paxos), are at the southern end of the Adriatic, while Kythira is off the tip of the Peloponnese. While the Ottomans had conquered most of Greece, they failed to permanently hold the Ionian Islands that had remained in Venetian hands for some four hundred years. The British colonial guide to the islands was not exactly flattering about the population, quoting the view that 'Their nobles are without honour, their merchants are without integrity, and their peasantry ignorant and degraded to the most abject degree'. However, their 'debased character' was apparently because they 'have been long subject to the demoralising influence of despotism.'[4] This, of course, was rapidly cured under British rule. What the locals thought of this analysis is not recorded!

Ionian Islands (From Holland's Travels, 1815)

Napoleon sent General Gentili to occupy the islands with a force of two thousand men. The small Venetian garrison did not resist, and the Dalmatian soldiers were shipped home. Rear Admiral Brueys had brought a French fleet into the Adriatic of six ships of the line and three frigates, which spent a month in Corfu and later visited Venice. Gentili soon fell ill, and General Louis Chabot replaced him in November 1797 for what looked like a peaceful posting. Chabot was an officer in the Maison du Roi and Poitou Regiment before the revolution. He progressed in the revolutionary army at Lille and Antwerp before achieving the rank of Brigadier General in the Vendee uprising. He became a general of division under Napoleon and commanded the 1st Division in the Italian campaign.

The French organised the islands as the départements Mer-Égée, Ithaque, and Corcyre. They also acquired some Venetian warships, which were sent to Corfu, including *Eolo* (70) and *Gloria* (66). These were renamed *Robert* and *Banel*, respectively. Brueys returned to Toulon in February 1798, leaving *Sandos* (64), *Lonato* (40), *Rivoli* (16), *Mondovi* (16) and *Cybele* (12) at Corfu. *Laharpe* (74), *Stengel* (64), *Beyrand* (64) and three smaller ships were left at Ancona.

Louis François Jean Chabot 1757-1837
(Unknown painter, public domain)

It is tempting to ask why Napoleon wanted these islands that were far from French territory. Napoleon wrote in his diary, 'I think that henceforth the chief maxim of the French Republic should be never to give up Corfu, Zante, etc.... With Malta and Corfu we should soon be masters of the Mediterranean.' Writing to his brother Joseph, then King of Naples, he said, 'Corfu is so important to me that its loss would deal a fatal blow to my plans. The Adriatic would be closed, and your kingdom would have on its left flank a port where the enemy could assemble to attack you. You must regard it as more valuable than Sicily. Mark my words: in the current situation in Europe the worst misfortune that can happen to me is to lose Corfu.'[5] Some historians have speculated that he viewed them as a base for an invasion and dismemberment of the Ottoman Empire, along with Austria and Russia. The islands, particularly Corfu, would be a convenient jumping-off point for an invasion down the traditional invasion route from Albania to Istanbul via Egnatia. Aside from this possibility, Corfu is also a formidable fortress, and the Ionian Islands came with ports on the coast of Epirus: Parga, Preveza, Vonitza and Butrinto.

Pre-revolutionary France had good relations with the Francophile Ottoman Sultan Selim III, who had helped rebuild the Ottoman navy and reorganise the artillery. The Sultan was not ideologically hostile to revolutionary France. Still, a new Tsar had improved Ottoman relations with Russia, and Napoleon's agents working with the *ayans* made Selim suspicious of Napoleon's motives. Napoleon's excursion to Egypt, via Malta, in July 1798 confirmed these suspicions. Despite Napoleon's attempt to describe this as restoring Ottoman rule from the Mameluks, it achieved what had seemed impossible—a Russo-Ottoman alliance. The Ottomans declared war on France on 11 September 1798, confiscating French property, and the Sultan imprisoned his pro-French ministers. Tsar Paul was equally upset with the French over Malta. He was the Grand Master of the Knights of Malta.

Sultan Selim III (*Life on the Bosphorus*, 1895)

One Ottoman leader the French had been courting from their Ionian Island base was Ali Pasha, who controlled the mainland opposite the islands, operating semi-autonomously from the directions of the Porte. General Chabot (other sources say it was Gentili[6]) had reported that Ali was full of admiration for Napoleon and received a French delegation at his Ioannina headquarters. He even bestowed a wife (probably his illegitimate daughter) on a French officer. In private talks with Chabot, he asked for weapons, technical assistance, and access for warships around Corfu. Chabot even agreed to ferry Ali's Albanian troops, led by the colourfully-named Yusuf Arab the Blood Drinker, through the straits for a surprise attack on the prosperous town of Nivitza. Some six thousand civilians were said to have been slaughtered, some roasted alive and impaled, and the rest sent to serve on Ali's farms[7].

The Russians enter the Mediterranean

General Chabot's quiet posting ended with the Russo-Ottoman alliance. In early September 1798, the Russian Black Sea Fleet, under Admiral Ushakov, brought six ships of the line (including *Sv. Pavel* (84), *Sv. Troitsa* (72), and *Sv. Petr* (74)) and ten frigates and corvettes into the Mediterranean, with experienced officers and crews.

Fyodor Ushakov was born in 1745. His father was a sergeant in the Preobrazhensky Regiment of the Russian Imperial guards, but he chose the navy and served on a galley in the Baltic. In 1768 he transferred to the Black Sea, commanding Catherine the Great's yacht. After 1783, he supervised the construction of naval bases at Sevastopol and Kherson. He made his name as a naval commander during the Russo-Turkish War (1787–92), defeating the Ottomans at Fidonisi (1788), Kerch Strait (1790), Tendra (1790), and Cape Kaliakra (1791).

Admiral Fyodor Ushakov (Peter Bajanov, public domain)

The Russian Navy in this period had developed from its early days under Peter the Great with its own shipbuilding capacity, supplemented by captured vessels, not least thirty-four taken from Sweden, which constituted a fifth of the fleet. A Russian fleet under Alexis Orlov had defeated the Ottomans in

1770 and encouraged revolts in Greece and the Balkans. By the 1780s, the Russian Navy was the fourth largest in the world, with 28 ships of the line and 149 frigates. However, this was primarily a Baltic fleet. The Black Sea Fleet had only been created in 1782, with its bases in the newly conquered lands at Nikolaev (Mykolaiv), Kherson and Sevastopol. These were all a long way from St. Petersburg, with unique theatre requirements which allowed commanders some autonomy.

For the 1798 campaign the Russians agreed to support the Ottomans in defending their territories against the French fleet, and Ushakov arrived at the Straits on 4 September with his fleet. Ushakov, the former scourge of the Ottomans, was now wined and dined in Istanbul, hailed as 'Pasha-Ushak'. He had six months of supplies on board, which indicated a serious campaign was planned. It was agreed that the main part of the fleet would be sent to liberate the Ionian Islands while keeping a weather eye on the pro-French tendencies of Ali Pasha. The proclamation to the population of the Ionian Islands from the Tsar suggested that the Ragusan Republic could be a model for the Islands, and the Orthodox Patriarch in Istanbul stirred up religious sentiment. As Saul puts it, 'It was indeed a sign of the unusual times that the absolutist Tsar of Russia advocated a republic and the Turkish Sultan backed a call for renewed Christian fervour!'[8]

Ushakov had an experienced fleet with veteran officers, including Greeks such as Klopakis, Alexiano and Metaxa, and British including Messer and Baillie, who also helped with liaison. However, ship construction was ineffective due to poor-quality timber, and several ships lacked the protective copper sheathing necessary in warm waters. Nelson is quoted as describing a Russian ship of the line thus: 'He says a gale of wind would have sunk the ship.'[9] Ushakov's orders were to join with the British fleet under Nelson and capture Malta and the Ionian Islands. An Ottoman squadron, under Abdülkadir Beg (Kadir Bey), joined him with four ships of the line, six frigates and four corvettes. Ushakov summarised his first impressions to the Russian Envoy in Istanbul: 'I have become well acquainted with the commander of the Turkish squadron, Pasha or Vice-Admiral Kadir-Bey. He seems to be extremely gentle and a courteous man; and everything was decided by us in a friendly way.'[10]

The bulk of the combined fleet went north to the Ionian Islands, while the remainder joined the British blockade of Alexandria. This reinforcement was not welcomed by the British commander Samuel Hood, who described the Ottomans 'as horrid a set of allies as I ever saw.'

The French Ionian Islands garrison had grown to four thousand troops, but they were spread across the Islands. The British consul, Spiridion Foresti, reported they included three thousand French and one thousand Italian troops, although at least two hundred were hospitalised. French warships, including the frigate *la Brune*, visited the islands in March 1798; these ships were used to ferry reinforcements to individual garrisons, including sixteen cannons to Zante. Foresti also reported that the French dismissed most of the former Venetian garrison, despite their willingness to shift allegiances, and they were shipped to Cattaro. The French moved some artillery pieces from the forts to warships, a process described by Foresti as 'without any secrecy whatsoever; and in a word, everything is conducted with the utmost effrontery.'[11] They also removed guns from Venetian ships. The consul was optimistic about the islands' inhabitants revolting if British ships arrived, particularly in Zante, which had strong commercial links with Britain.

The Russian ships *Grigorii Velikia Armenii* (50) and *Stchastlivyi* (32) struck the southernmost island, Cerrigo, on 9 October, forcing the outnumbered French naval infantry to surrender. The joint Russo-Turkish fleet moved north, capturing Zante (24 October), then Cephalonia and Santa Maure. The main French force was concentrated at Corfu, which had well-fortified citadels and two warships in the harbour—the 74-gun *Généreux*, a survivor of the Battle of the Nile, and the British 50-gun *Leander*, which the French had captured. A four-month siege ensued in which the Russo-Ottoman forces attempted to starve the French out. A relief squadron was sent from Ancona with three thousand troops. However, only one of the three ex-Venetian ships of the line reached Corfu (*Stengel*). The commander decided he could not break into the harbour, so returned to Ancona.

After three months, Nelson asked for reinforcements to defend Sicily, where King Ferdinand of Naples had moved his court after the French forced him out of Naples. This court included Lady Hamilton, which may have influenced Nelson's priorities! For good reasons, these priorities were not shared by Ushakov and Kadir Bey, who were suspicious of British motives. In a letter to the Russian ambassador in Istanbul, Ushakov wrote, 'They have always wanted to take Corfu for themselves and wished to send us away under various pretexts, or by splitting us up reduce us to incapacity.'[12]

A renewed attack on the fortress island of Vido, opposite the citadel on Corfu, began on 28 February. A bombardment by eight hundred naval guns killed one-third of the six hundred French defenders and destroyed all their artillery. This was followed by the landing of one thousand Russian troops in the north and one thousand Ottoman soldiers in the west. Most of the remaining French troops surrendered, including their commander, General Piverton. The Russians had to protect the prisoners from the Ottoman soldiers, who had no intention of giving quarter. Even though the attacks on the main fortress had failed, the French were short of supplies and asked for terms, which included their repatriation to Toulon. *Généreux* escaped the rather loose Russo-Turkish blockade and attempted to return with reinforcements, but it was too late. *Leander* was captured and returned to the British. The siege is dramatised in the Russian 1953 film, *Korabli shturmuyut bastion* (Attack from the Sea).[13]

Nelson did succeed in keeping the Russians away from Malta, again acting more for King Ferdinand than the British government, which viewed the island as an unnecessary expense. He refused assistance from Ushakov, writing, 'The Russians shall never take the island.' Elements of the Russo-Turkish fleet, including two Russian ships of the line, two frigates, and an Ottoman ship of the line and frigate, made an attempt on Ancona on 17 May. The garrison refused a call to surrender, and an exchange of fire with shore batteries did minor damage to each side.

Ali Pasha and the French

On the subject of allies, even when war broke out in September 1798, Ali Pasha communicated with the French, possibly even offering to join them in return for the island of Lefkas (Lefkada) and ten thousand French troops. An offer the French commander, General Chabot, refused. So, taking control of the Ottoman war effort on the mainland, Ali Pasha mobilised twenty thousand men and besieged the port of Butrint.

Ali Pasha's fort at Butrint (Author)

Chabot cut his losses and retreated to Corfu. At Preveza, the four-hundred-strong French force, commanded by General Lasalcette and a local militia of around six hundred men, built a line of defence close to the ancient city of Nicopolis. On 23 October 1798, Ali brought a seven-thousand-strong force (one-third cavalry) to attack the position, but his infantry and artillery failed to break the lines. It took two cavalry charges led by Ali's son Muktar to defeat them. Ali watched the battle from the same spot Emperor Augustus had watched his fleet destroy Anthony and Cleopatra at Actium in 31 BC. The now-customary slaughter of Greek prisoners took place in the town of Preveza—an event that would be remembered in song and serve as a rallying call during the later Greek revolution. Others were dispersed or sold into slavery. Twelve French grenadiers and officers (other sources say 147[14]) were sent in chains to Istanbul.

Vonitsa fell quickly, but Parga was a tougher prospect. Parga is built on a rock which juts out into the sea and is joined to the mainland by a peninsula. It also had a castle built by the Venetians with thirty cannons and a militia of some five hundred men. The strong defences and the population's loyalty meant that Ali's entreaties to slaughter the French garrison received the reply, 'Your too lively examples lead us all to prefer a glorious and free death to an infamous and tyrannical slavery.'

The arrival of the Russo-Ottoman fleet thwarted Ali's ambition to grab Santa Maura, and the Pargians understandably decided that Russian protection was a better option than Ali Pasha. Ushakov sent a small force to take control of the port. Nonetheless, Ali came out of the conflict in good standing. Nelson called him 'the hero of Epirus', and the Sultan made him a Pasha of Three Tails. He also used one of his French prisoners, Colonel Charbonnel, to establish a military school. Ali's ambitions were not limited to the Ionian Islands.

The War of Second Coalition 1799-1801

The alliance of Britain, Russia and the Ottoman Empire that brought a Russian fleet to the Adriatic turned into a broader coalition in the spring of 1799, partly due to the French expansion of its satellite republics and Napoleon's invasion of Egypt. That campaign is outside the scope of this study. Even though the Ottomans only nominally ruled the Mameluke state, they viewed Napoleon's descent on Egypt as a hostile act. This broke the positive relations between the Ottomans and the French, diverting ships and men from the Adriatic to the Egyptian coast.

Ushakov was promoted to full admiral as a reward for capturing the Ionian Islands, which did not solve his new challenges. He had to politically organise the islands, maintain good relations with the Ottomans and British, and maintain a rotting fleet in a harbour ill-equipped for the task. Like other commanders in the Mediterranean, he suffered from long lines of communication. He had to use Russian and Turkish marines to garrison the islands while he awaited Russian troops, some of which were then diverted to Suvorov's army in Italy. Finally, on 1 November 1800, a noble-led republic was agreed upon between the Russians and Ottomans, and called the 'Republic of the Seven United Islands' (Septinsular Republic).

Flag of the Septinsular Republic 1800-1807 (Orange Tuesday, public domain)

The Austrians needed some convincing and British cash to join the coalition. Still, many in Vienna had regarded the Treaty of Campo Formio as simply an armistice. This faction did not include Archduke Charles, who headed the peace faction arguing that the proposed army reforms were not completed. As Austria was providing 80 per cent of allied manpower, this was not encouraging. Archduke Charles was the third son of Emperor Leopold II. He began his military career in the revolutionary wars, commanding a brigade at Jemappes in 1792. He became a field marshal and later commander in chief, fighting in most of the Austrian campaigns against Napoleon. He was respected both as a commander and as a reformer of the Austrian army, and was considered one of Napoleon's more formidable opponents.

While the French were outnumbered, their army organisation remained superior in operating flexible, large, all-arms formations. In Italy, the Russian General Suvorov was given command of Austrian troops supporting his corps. Outnumbering the French two to one, he moved across northern Italy and captured Milan on 29 April. A political falling-out over restoring the Kingdom of Sardinia seriously damaged relations between the Austrians and the Russians. Some assert that Suvorov could have gone on to invade France. However, Rothenberg argues that Suvorov's reputation was inflated based on his wars against the Ottomans[15]. Furthermore, the Russians were advancing slowly, with few support services; their tactics were crude, based on the cult of the bayonet, which resulted in casualties twice those of the French. In August, Suvorov was ordered into Switzerland, leaving the Austrian army commanded by Melas to face a reinforced French army under Joubert. Melas defeated the

French at Novi, forcing them back to Genoa. Suvorov slowly advanced into Switzerland but fell out with Archduke Charles over future cooperation. In October, he retired to winter quarters near Augsburg.

Ushakov was ordered to support Russian operations in Italy. He dispatched two squadrons to patrol the Adriatic and blockade French ports. In May 1799, the British (possibly Irish)-born Captain Henry Baillie, serving in the Russian fleet, landed in Brindisi with six hundred Russian marines. He united with the Neapolitan militia to capture several cities and entered Naples on 14 June. While supporting these operations in Italy, Ushakov was reinforced by a Russian squadron from the Baltic fleet under Vice Admiral Kartsov. However, Ushakov and Nelson clashed over strategy, and the allied Turkish squadron returned to Istanbul after crew disturbances in Palermo. The failure of an Anglo-Russian expedition to northern Holland added to the tensions between the Russians and their allies, and the Tsar ordered his troops home.

A small Austrian flotilla also took part in the Austrian campaign in Italy, moving down the coast from Venice with two fourteen-gun xebecs and twelve gunboats. They joined the siege of Ancona, but relations between the allies were poor and contributed to a wider breakdown. Rome had been occupied by Neapolitan troops, the Papal ports of Civita Vecchia by the British, and Ancona by the Russians. In response, Austria marched into Ancona, expelling the Russian forces, which unsurprisingly led to Tsar Paul breaking off all diplomatic relations with the Austrians. Napoleon also worked to turn him against the British with a vague promise to hand over Malta, knowing that the British were about to take possession.

Ushakov received the orders to return home and concentrated his fleet, which in any case needed extensive renovation and reinforcement, at Corfu. Some ships had to be left there for local repairs under the command of Voinovich, who was tasked to preserve order until reinforcements could be sent. Ushakov sailed for Sevastopol on 17 July 1800.

The British thought there was still life in the Second Coalition and had a high opinion of the improved Austrian army. These hopes were to be dashed by the return of Napoleon from Egypt and his appointment as First Consul in November 1799. He offered to open peace negotiations with the Austrians; but, boosted by some modest gains in Italy and British support, the Austrians planned new offensives for 1800. In Italy, these started well, with Genoa falling in June 1800. However, Napoleon took the Reserve Army and moved through the Alps into Lombardy, cutting the Austrian lines of communication. At the

Battle of Marengo (14 June 1800), Napoleon defeated General Melas, who signed an armistice and abandoned Lombardy. Despite losses in Germany, the Austrian emperor was persuaded to continue the war with British subsidies that paid for thirty thousand German troops. A new offensive in Germany led by the 18-year-old Archduke John collapsed at Hohenlinden (3 December 1800). With the Austrian army deserting, the emperor was forced to agree to the Peace of Luneville in February 1801, which confirmed the provisions of Campo Formio.

The Second Coalition was at an end—Napoleon was back on the Adriatic coast, and the Austrians withdrew from Ancona. Even Britain was forced to rethink its strategy, and the Peace of Amiens (March 1802) ended most of the conflicts between the major powers. All sides needed more than a breather. Britain had accumulated a mountain of debt and growing unrest at home. France had achieved its natural borders, although Britain's dominance on the seas had halted Napoleon's dream of empire. France also needed time to recover and demonstrate that nearly a decade of war could bring a prosperous peace.

In practice, Britain and France manoeuvred for an advantage during the peace. France quietly annexed Italian states, and the British held onto Malta as an important staging post for later actions in the Adriatic. The assassination of Tsar Paul in March 1801 brought Tsar Alexander to the throne. He had no pretensions towards Malta, and while he did not formally break with Napoleon, he quietly advised the British he would have no problem if they wanted to retain the island.

CHAPTER THREE

SMALL WARS IN THE BALKANS

A key feature of the Napoleonic Wars was the increased size of the armies deployed by the leading powers. At Austerlitz in 1805, 73,200 French faced 85,400 allies. By the time of Borodino, the armies had grown to 133,000 French against 120,000 Russians. This growing deployment of manpower reached its apogee at Leipzig, where 195,000 French faced 356,000 allies.

In the Balkans, large-scale battles were rare; this was primarily a small-war conflict. In *On War*, Clausewitz described five conditions for the successful prosecution of guerrilla warfare, all of which apply to the Balkans. In particular, the countryside had to be mountainous, forested, or otherwise rough and inaccessible. The population's character also had to be suited to armed resistance. This chapter will look at some of these small-war conflicts and the local military organisations.

The Military Border

The Habsburgs had organised their border defence system since the sixteenth century. It stretched from the Adriatic to Hungary, some one thousand kilometres in length, with over 120 forts and watchtowers. The defence was formalised into the Military Border (Militargrenze), thirty to one hundred kilometres deep, populated by soldier-colonists who were given land and other privileges in return for military service. By this period, the troops were no longer simply a frontier militia but an important component of the Habsburg armed forces. These "Grenzers" were not serfs, as in civil Croatia behind them. This status was important to them and built a dynastic loyalty to the Habsburg emperor.

The Military Border was still suffering the aftereffects of the Austro-Turkish War (1788-91) when the War of the First Coalition broke out in 1792. Losses weakened the regiments, and units had to remain vigilant against Ottoman incursions, particularly on the Bosnian border. Only a couple of composite battalions and free corps were scraped together, and these suffered heavy losses. The Treaty of Campo Formio meant a return to the Military Border, which had suffered economic disruption due to the wars and harvest failure. Administrative changes renumbered the seventeen infantry regiments, designating them as National-Gränz-Infantrie Regimenter. We will look in detail at the organisation of Austrian forces later, but at this stage, the changes were largely cosmetic and did little for military effectiveness. General De Vins, who had led a Croatian corps in the war against the Ottomans, was 'appalled by the evidence of dire want, poverty, and neglect' among the Grenzers.[1] He died before his reform proposals could be considered. Still, his replacement General Alvintzy, and later General Colloredo, attempted to reduce taxes and raise the level of education. However, the Austrians had more territory to garrison after they took over Venetian possessions. Even with immigration from Ottoman areas, there was insufficient manpower.

Karlstadt (Karlovac) Castle. Military Border district headquarters. (Author)

On the Military Border during the War of the Second Coalition, the Habsburgs now benefited from the alliance with the Ottomans because fewer troops were required to maintain the defences. This released some thirty-six battalions for active service, plus a hussar regiment and two battalions of sharpshooters, a total of thirty thousand men. Some twenty-four Grenzer battalions fought in Italy and Switzerland, although casualty replacements had to be recruited from outside the Military Border.

Following the collapse of the Second Coalition, Archduke Charles was appointed as President of the Hofkeriggsrat (War Council) and minister of war. He began extensive political and military reforms, again facing considerable internal opposition. He did improve the administration, but money was short, and he struggled to reform recruitment and conditions for both junior officers and the enlisted ranks. Plans to create a larger standing army with divisions and corps floundered. Efforts to establish the nucleus of an Adriatic fleet in Senj and Karlobag to challenge piracy had also ground to a halt during the wars against the French.

In the Military Border, there were demands to disband the institution following mutinies in June 1800. These were resisted, and Charles appointed Archduke Ludwig and a commission to investigate and make recommendations for reform. This commission argued that attempts to make the Grenzer regular infantry were contrary to their customs and temperament, and that they should return to their traditional light infantry role. They linked these changes to economic reforms and a new code of basic laws for the Border that recognised that drill and prolonged training ruined the economy. Conditions in the Karlstadt Border were particularly harsh, where the land was less fertile than in the Banal and Warasdin districts. However, the former also benefited from not having to maintain a cordon watch over the Ottoman frontier. The overall lack of skilled artisans and profitable trade meant the Border relied on the government for relief, as one writer concluded 'that neither manufacture nor trade can prosper under military rule'.[2] Important though these issues were, the critical factor limiting the Military Border was manpower. In 1799, 823,950 people lived in the Military Border, including 101,902 of military age. Three years later, this had halved, not least because of a thirty-eight per cent casualty rate (thirty-eight thousand men) during the coalition wars. There had been thirty different schemes to reform the Military Border in the past century; none of these reforms had been implemented before Archduke Charles resigned in 1804.

The War of the Third Coalition saw forty-eight thousand Grenzer mobilised, and twenty-three battalions fought in northern Italy. After Austerlitz, French troops under General Sarras advanced through Istria into Croatia, threatening Karlstadt. The remaining Grenzer home guards were ill-equipped to resist them. Returning Grenzer prisoners of war worried the Austrian police, who feared 'many who have succumbed to French influence and are spreading false doctrines.'[3] In response, Archduke Charles was restored to continue his reforms after the war. The emperor signed a new code in August 1807, which sought to lessen the burden on the Grenzer, including some security of tenure over their land, limiting communal labour, and making provisions for uniforms and equipment. It also aimed at maintaining a ready supply of troops. The establishment of a regiment was set at 2,570 officers and men, including an administrative section of 228 personnel. A special military school was established for officers in Graz (Granz-Verwaltungs Institut). Tactically, the new code and field regulations aimed to return the Grenzer to light infantry functions, and drill stressed marksmanship and skirmishing.

The Treaty of Schonbrunn resulted in six Karlstadt and Banal regiments being transferred to French service on 1 December 1809. The Austrians removed modern muskets and artillery, and generally, the Grenzer welcomed the transfer with the hope that their military burdens would be relieved. The Austrian claims of the Grenzer 'undying devotion and loyalty' was simply a patriotic legend. However, despite infrastructure and other improvements, Napoleon viewed the border as the Austrians had, as a barrier to protect his empire's flank, so its military considerations had priority. The French governor of the newly formed Illyrian Provinces, Marshal Marmont, strongly supported the Grenzer system, although Napoleon was less convinced. He initially refused requests for new muskets until the Turkish threat became clearer. After several reviews, Napoleon eventually gave in, although Marmont was replaced by General Bertrand in April 1811. The Grenzer were formally incorporated as light troops in French service. French became the official language of command, and two hundred Grenzer boys were sent to France for a military education.

With the fall of Napoleon in 1815, the Grenzer returned to Austrian service and their traditional role, resisting Bosnian incursions and providing troops to bolster Austrian armies elsewhere.

The Ottoman Frontier

Facing the Austrian Military Border in Croatia was the Ottoman province (vilayet or eyalet) of Bosnia. The governor was appointed by the Sultan and had the title of Beglerbeg, held the highest rank of pasha called a 'three-tailed pasha', and was usually based in Travnik. There was little consistency, with nine different governors during this period and thirty between 1730 and 1798. The province was then subdivided into districts (*sancaklar*), which changed boundaries many times over the century, having both judicial and military divisions. In this period, there were four *sandcaks*, Bosnia, Hercegovina, Zvornik and Klis, but structures changed every time a new governor was appointed. Even the boundaries of the Bosnian governor could change with each appointment. Hickok argues[4] that this makes more sense than it might at first appear. There were wide variations in the quality of personnel, and relationships were more personal than in the western institutional model. Flexibility was a deliberate state policy, not one based on resistance from local elites.

The Ottomans were more religiously tolerant than their Christian opponents, which meant that most people in the Balkans retained their religious affiliations and, through the *Millet* system, had a significant degree of autonomy within their religious community[5]. However, in Bosnia, large-scale conversions occurred after Ottoman occupation, supplemented by Muslim refugees from Christian lands. This resulted in a Muslim ruling class primarily of Slavic origin, although Orthodox peasants still outnumbered them. Modern scholarship has moved away from the concept of a surviving pre-conquest Bogomil nobility[6] towards the awarding of *ocakliks*. These appear to have been an annual salary rather than a hereditary land holding, as previously thought[7].

In addition to the usual military organisation, the border areas in Bosnia included military *kapitanates*, increasingly hereditary military chiefs whose duties were to guard the frontier and the lines of communication. Thirty-eight of these areas had around twenty-four thousand soldiers attached to them by 1800. Militia commands had a variety of companies attached, depending on the area. Titles can be confusing, as *kapudans* could also have the title *aga*. Typically, each company was commanded by an *aga* or *sertop* for an artillery unit and *dizdar* for a garrison unit. There was an executive officer called a *kethüda*, which in the Bosnian militia was the second-in-command and administrative officer. There was usually an *alemdar*, and a *cavus*; other troops singled out for higher pay were called either *serhad* or *oda basi*.

There are few signs of padding out units with superfluous posts, which indicates that the Bosnian militia was well-organised and commanded. Appointment records suggest that while offices could be passed on within a family, they were not hereditary. Promotions had to be justified and reviewed by the governor and in Istanbul. The military was also more consistent organisationally than civilian structures, implying a higher degree of control than previously thought. This was primarily achieved through funding as the militia outnumbered government troops sent to the frontiers. Kapudans were also popular with the people because these commanders had a stake in the area, unlike external appointees, who enriched themselves for a few years and then moved on. Larger towns like Sarajevo and Mostar also had a degree of autonomy from the governor.

The wars of the 18th century bore down heavily on Bosnia, both in military casualties and from the plague and other diseases. Agriculture was disrupted, and the Muslim population lost greater numbers than others as only they fought in the Ottoman armies. The growth of tax farming estates (*čiftlik*) also placed extra demands on the peasants, who were reduced to little more than subsistence—aggravated by wartime confiscation of livestock and foodstuffs. Tax farming also began complicating militia funding, weakening the governor's position with the militias. The militarised provincial administration levied emergency taxes to fund local fortifications and even for wars further east in the Balkans. Many in Bosnia complained that Istanbul officials neglected this frontier. An Ottoman Bosnian writer in 1810 penned a petition to the Sultan in prose[8]:

> Bosnia is the head of your frontier
> On one side is the river Sava
> On three sides flows the infidel lava
> So you know that, burning sunshine…
> We waged war for the borderland
> We guarded the Bosnian highland…
> Fifteen thousand martyrs we gave
> But no one cares for that today…
> Sultan, ruler, burning sunshine.

The Habsburg wars also increased hostility toward Christian peasants (mainly Catholics) as the potential enemy within. The Franciscan Order, which had monasteries in Bosnia, regularly refused Austrian requests for intelligence, fearful of retaliation if discovered. However, they occasionally gave in to pressure. For example, in 1785, an Austrian lieutenant travelled through Bosnia disguised as a Franciscan friar, staying in monasteries. This was part of an extensive intelligence-gathering operation in this period.

Despite all this, Bosnia's Christian population recovered from one hundred and forty-three thousand in 1732 to four hundred thousand in 1817. Bosnia was better governed than neighbouring Serbia, although there is little evidence of large-scale migration. Natural growth indicates a functioning economy, even if one characterised by poverty, with religious toleration. This was a period of economic growth when trade between the Ottoman Empire and Europe increased rapidly. This economic contact contributed to the growth of national movements, initially largely cultural, but later leading to armed rebellion. Visitors to Bosnia during this period noted that Christians dressed like Muslims, other than small details. There was also a significant Jewish population, with as many as two thousand in Sarajevo dominating the cloth trade. Jews ran an early metal foundry that made weapons and equipment for the Ottoman army. There were also around eight thousand gipsies in Bosnia in 1808 who were predominantly Muslim and generally better treated than in Christian lands.

A small war continued between the major conflicts, with both sides raiding across the border. Military salaries were never high, and raiding offered an opportunity to gain wealth through booty. Both sides turned a blind eye to this lucrative form of raiding, with weapons, grain, livestock and enslaved people being the main forms of plunder, sold in local markets. Ransoms could amount to more than the booty a soldier could carry, and a payment system developed. Officers attracted the highest payments, and even regular soldiers drew significant sums.

The last major war in 1788 had a political dimension in that Austria and Russia agreed on a plan to divide the Ottoman Balkans, with Austria getting Bosnia. Austria hoped for an uprising from Bosnian Christians, but both Christians and Muslims put up stiff resistance. Christian troops were attracted to military service in Ottoman garrisons (like *martolos* units) because it was less onerous work than farming, and had higher wages and tax exemptions. For Bosnia, the main threat shifted from the Austrians to the Russians in the early 19th century, undermining common interests.

Traditional accounts of the Balkans often describe the Ottoman years as a cultural wasteland. This is simple prejudice, as the architecture, poetry, and other literary works demonstrate. Bosnian Muslims were noticeably less strict in their adherence to Islamic practices, particularly the drinking of alcohol. Outside the religious establishment, the dervish orders came early to Bosnia, with the Bektashi order influential among the janissaries. The arrival of the French on the border and the rise of autonomous Serbia undoubtedly increased the sense of being surrounded, which increased social-religious polarisation. However, this was not always the case in Bosnia. Borders were a linguistic frontier, with state officials rarely being able to speak the language of the other side, be that Latin or Ottoman Turkish. Border officials played an important role as translators, and Hungarian became the local language of diplomacy. Both sides employed spies and informants, developing intelligence and remarkably accurate maps, including fortifications.

Dervish tekija near Blagaj in Bosnia (Author)

On the Adriatic frontier, the Ottomans were concerned that the French would use the Ionian Islands as a jumping-off point for an invasion of Albania or the Morea. This concern predated Napoleon's invasion of Egypt, conventionally considered the breaking point of previous good Franco-Ottoman relations. They turned a blind eye to the provisioning of the islands as part of a cautious diplomatic stance and even considered the idea of purchasing the islands[9]. This approach ended with the Egyptian invasion, which pushed the Ottomans into an almost unheard-of alliance with the Russians.

The compromise reached on the islands' status after they were captured was fraught with misunderstandings. The Ottomans viewed them as a tributary state, whereas the Russians regarded that status as tokenistic. The Treaty of Amiens also failed to mention Ottoman suzerainty. The token Ottoman force on Corfu was supposed to be paid and provisioned by the islanders, but this rarely happened. Russian recruitment of native troops and sailors, achieved by paying twice the wage of Ottoman soldiers, upset the Ottomans. The Ottomans also viewed the islands as a buffer state, although an expensive one. The tribute never covered the cost of provisioning the Russian fleet, draining the Ottoman campaign fund. This added to the strains in relations with the Russians that resulted in war and the return of the French in 1807.

While each of the Ottoman regions on the border operated differently, they all reflected the disintegration of central rule from Istanbul and the challenges faced by Sultan Selim III in reforming the empire. However, there were many connections between different parts of the empire, with officials moving around frontier areas during their careers. This is common in most empires throughout history and helped develop an understanding of remote areas. Population movements or forced migration were also not unusual. For example, Habsburg advances and then retreats brought Serbs into the Military Border, and their place was taken in Kosovo by Albanians, sowing the seed of conflict today. However, the scale of migration is probably exaggerated by both Serbian and Albanian nationalist historians[10].

Fortifications

Fortifications on both sides of the border had been crucial to the small wars on the frontier since the Ottoman invasion. They became the visible points of encounter, often changing hands after a major conflict. They were key elements of the maps prepared by both sides, emphasising the understanding of geography and topography in campaigns. As the borderline settled, both sides built fortifications to secure strongpoints and to serve as bases for offensive operations. Larger strategic towns had traditional stone fortresses, such as Bihac, Gradiska, Dubica and Belgrade on the Ottoman side, and Cetingrad, Petrovaradin and Karlstadt in Croatia. However, more minor fortifications were important in prosecuting the small wars.

Petrovaradin Fortress on the Danube (Author)

Fortresses were expensive to build and garrison, so large-angle bastioned forts of the type common in western Europe were rare. Adapting earlier fortifications, including medieval castles, was a cheaper option, and archaeologists have identified later Ottoman additions[11]. An officer in the British military mission to the Ottomans was generally scathing about the maintenance of Ottoman fortifications. He said, 'Little or no attention is paid to the keeping of them in repair; and it is very much to be doubted whether they would be of any efficacy in case of foreign attack and invasion.'[12] Forts were built on rivers, often next to bridges, not only for defensive purposes but also because they were an essential part of Ottoman campaign logistics. Supplies like the giant Ottoman cannonballs were much easier to move on boats than on the inadequate road system.

We know more about the stone fortresses because there are archaeological remains, unlike wooden structures. The typical Ottoman fort was the *palanka*, a small palisaded earthwork fortification built from timber (usually oak) with vertical layers filled with mortar. A ditch typically surrounded it, with a bridge and watchtower built at the entrance. There would be timber buildings housing both barracks and storerooms for munitions and food. Palankas could also be used to extend existing fortifications, such as in Belgrade. Because of the building materials, few palankas survive to this day. Still, archaeologists have found evidence of these structures from the fourteenth to the late nineteenth century[13].

Fortress building and repair were important to the local economy and paid well. Ottoman carpenters working on palankas could earn three times the typical salary.[14] However, forts could also damage the local economy, because they were a target of warfare and the land around them had to be prioritised for defence. This meant rivers could be diverted and swampland left uncultivated. Defence-related activities also damaged the environment through deforestation, which accelerated the spread of swamps.

Palanka Fort (Marsigli, public domain)

The long wars against the Habsburgs caused the Ottomans to strengthen the border fortifications in the 18th century. Twenty-eight forts and eight palankas were built along the Sava and Una rivers in the first half of the century. Another building programme began in 1742 and was concluded by the end of the century. Selim III brought in French engineers to advise on modernising forts, and new fortifications were built on the Montenegrin and Wallachian borders. Wooden walls may appear anachronistic by 18th-century standards when we think of the massive Vauban forts on the French frontier. However, Vauban's influence can be seen in the geometric designs of palankas such as Fethulislam (Kladovo) on the Danube. Artillery was rarely used in the raiding of the small war and even when it was, the ditch and earthworks still provided a useful defence. There are many period maps and drawings of Habsburg, Venetian, and Ottoman fortresses on the border, although these need to be viewed with some caution. These are rarely scale drawings; rather, they are often simply an artistic depiction to celebrate a victory. Nonetheless, they indicate that the fortress was often the centrepiece for marking frontiers and possessions[15].

Civilian buildings also had to be ready for war. In the Austrian Military Border and Ottoman Serbia, the Grenzer lived in family groups known as *zadruga*. There was typically a central room with sleeping chambers off to the side. Muslim houses were generally square, while Christians preferred oblong structures. Some evidence suggests that buildings were not entirely built of stone for defence, unlike those further south in Herzegovina, because the ever-present raiding and destruction made such an investment pointless[16]. Family ties were all-important, so the zadruga could expand to form a small village. In Ottoman Serbia, families would elect representatives to serve on the district council (*knezevina*), which dealt with the landlords and Ottoman officials. It was the zadruga that preserved Serbian traditions, more so than the Orthodox Church, whose Greek hierarchy was distant from the peasants[17].

Border conflicts

The 18th century is often described as the period of Ottoman decline, although modern scholarship argues this is a simplified description. It was a period of contraction, but in the Balkans, the border was relatively stable in our period. In many ways, internal challenges were more significant, although if force failed to put down a revolt, then bribery or promotion could be used. The aim was usually to increase prestige, not topple the Sultan. While revolts happened in all parts of the empire, those on the border were more dangerous as the rebels could often count on external support. The concept of the flexible border and the *gazi* state expanding the borders of Islam had disappeared with the delineation of the border in the 18th century. The Ottomans still adopted a flexible approach to border administration, with different systems to reflect local circumstances.

The Military Border that separated Ottoman Serbia and Bosnia from the Habsburg lands had traditionally been the scene of the small war in between the major wars. As with other borders between empires, the inhabitants supplemented their meagre incomes by raiding. Casualties during raids could lead to blood feuds, a practice common in large parts of the Balkans, although less prevalent in Serbia. The raids were primarily economic, typically seizing livestock rather than attacking fortified places. Slavery was also an essential source of revenue, including ransoming prisoners. This started to decline in our period but was still significant, and the Ottomans had a different perception of the institution than their western counterparts.

One of the functions of the Austrian Military Border was to enforce quarantine arrangements to keep the plague and other diseases prevalent in the Ottoman lands from the Habsburg territory. However, this did not stop trade. For example, after the governor Mustafa Pasha expelled disruptive elements from Belgrade, the area became rich from swineherding. Annually, the pashalik made 1,300,000 florins (130,000 pounds sterling) in its trade with Austria alone[18]. This, along with reforms including a fixed tax rate and permission to repair churches and monasteries, encouraged Serbs in the Habsburg lands to return to Serbia.

During this period, the biggest military threat to those living in Serbia came from the neighbouring Ottoman Vidin, which today is in northern Bulgaria. Osman Pasvanoglu frequently sent brigands into the Belgrade district, pillaging villages and taking captives. Osman raided into Wallachia but rarely into Austria, as he benefited from trade across the border. Neighbouring pashas would, on occasion, mount larger punitive expeditions against Osman. These forces could involve several thousand troops on each side.

Osman Pasvanoglu ruled a vast territory from his base at Vidin on the Danube. Vidin had been a fortress and port of the Danube since Roman times. It was an important Ottoman border town, captured and recovered several times. It became part of the border with the Habsburgs again after the Treaty of Belgrade in 1739. Vidin along with Nigbolu (Nikopol), Ruscuk (Ruse) and Silistre (Silistra) formed the backbone of the Ottoman Danube defences, and Vidin's citadel was the region's headquarters. The outer fortifications were remodelled on the Vauban principles by the Habsburgs and completed by the Ottomans. Osman Pasvanoglu strengthened them further, supporting them with a flotilla of ships on the Danube. The Timar system appears to have declined more rapidly in this region, and the town became highly militarised with a large number of janissaries. Records show 5,440 men, although that probably included local troops, and they stopped rotating, taking roots locally[19]. Osman's father was one such janissary who took local roots. He and his father, before him, commanded the 31st Janissary Orta.

Osman Pasvanoglu (unknown painter, public domain)

Osman and his father were expelled from Vidin, and he was sentenced to death in 1787 for extortion and rebellion. However, he made himself useful in the war against Austria, and was reprieved and allowed to return to Vidin. His army included dissatisfied janissaries and local recruits (*yamaks*) as well as Albanians, Bosnians and Turks. They raided across the border into Wallachia and the neighbouring Ottoman regions of Belgrade to the west, ruled by Mustafa Pasha, and into eastern Bulgaria, governed by Ismail Tirsiniklioglu Agha. The Sultan ordered Ali Pasha to take an army north, and he routed Osman's army without destroying his power base. In February 1798, the Sultan sent an army of between forty thousand and eighty thousand men against Vidin, commanded by Grand Admiral Küçük Hüseyin Pasha. The army included contingents from all the surrounding areas, including Ali Pasha, but there was little enthusiasm for the siege, and discipline was poor. After eight months, Hüseyin abandoned the siege with significant casualties as his ships and troops were needed in the Mediterranean, given rumours of Napoleon's fleet assembling at Toulon[20].

Despite a pardon from the Sultan, Osman continued to stir up revolts and raid the surrounding areas. With no help from Istanbul, Mustafa Pasha armed the Serbian population of Belgrade. The janissaries revolted with Osman's support, executing Mustafa, and held the city in what became known as the 'reign of the *dayis*' until the winter of 1804-05. Napoleon sent a mission to persuade Osman to support France in 1801, and the Russians sought to establish an embassy in Vidin. However, neither appear to have aided him in any significant way. He resisted Ottoman reforms in his territory, increasing his popularity with the peasants and attracting Christians and Muslims to his cause. He had an effective spy network, modernised the fortress, repaired roads, and improved the cultural life of the area.

The successful janissary revolt resulted in further small-scale warfare across the region. The janissaries sought to recover land from the Sipahi and increased taxes on the Serbs. They also spread dissatisfaction into Bosnia, which led the Vali of Bosnia, Ebu Bekir Pasha, to threaten Belgrade with Ottoman and Serbian troops. Osman was unable to supply his allies in Belgrade, and the city fell. As Robert Zens concludes[21], without Osman's actions, Serbia would have remained peaceful, prosperous and loyal. Only when he made living conditions unbearable both for the Serbs, and the Ottomans loyal to the sultan, was there any sign of rebellion. What then began as a social uprising gradually grew into the larger conflict of the First Serbian Uprising in 1805. Zens argues that Osman prepared the groundwork for the Serbian Uprising in the same way that Ali Pasha laid the foundation for the Greek Revolution.

After Osman died in 1807, his successor Bayraktar Mustafa Pasha occupied eastern Bulgaria and marched through the Balkan Mountains into Thrace. He was a key player in the Ruscuk Committee, bringing his army to Istanbul in July 1808. This led to the deposing of Sultan Mustafa IV in favour of his son Mahmud II. In October 1808, Mustafa brought together a gathering of the ayans and governors who signed the *sened-i ittifak*, an agreement on military and administrative reform. However, this agreement collapsed following his death in a janissary rebellion in November. Mahmud II survived and went on to be a major reformer, westernising institutions and disbanding the janissaries in 1826.

The Austrians had traditionally exploited rebellions against Ottoman rule. Still, faced with the prospects of another war with France, the government refused requests for aid. However, cross-border links between the Orthodox communities were strong, and arms and supplies found their way across the border. In particular, the Karlstadt, Banal and Slavonian regiments resented the decision of the government to refuse aid. When the Ottomans regained the initiative, cross-border raids increased, resulting in the regiments being mobilised and limited reprisal raids authorised. When the Ottomans succeeded in putting down the Serbian uprising, refugees fled across the border. Equally, Grenzer deserters crossed the border to join Serbian insurgent groups that the Russians were arming. Some limited negotiations began with the Serbian leader Karadjordje, and food supplies followed. The Austrians wanted to remain on good terms with the Ottomans and Russians. However, their primary concern was the risk that the Serbian revolt could become a broader Balkan revolt. A small mutiny in a Banat regiment in June 1808 reinforced these concerns.

The French became a player in the military border when they acquired the provinces of Venetia, Istria and Dalmatia in 1806. The French and Ottomans had returned to good relations in this period, and Napoleon sent assistance to the Sultan for local rebellions in Serbia and Hercegovina. In 1808, the French sent an expeditionary force to relieve the Ottoman pasha Hadži-beg-Rizvanbegović, besieged in the fortress of Hutovo. This could be a two-way street, as in 1809, when Napoleon encouraged the Bosnians to raid Habsburg Slavonia while the French were at war with the Austrians. The creation of the Illyrian Provinces in 1809 brought even more French involvement in the military border, including the transfer of six Karlstadt and Banal regiments to French service.

The French quickly discovered that centuries of small-scale warfare were not simply a Habsburg problem. Faced with regular raids from Bosnia, Marshal Marmont led a punitive expedition into Bosnia in late 1809. The Aga of Bihac led a small Bosnian force against them. Although easily dispersed, the cavalry impressed the French veterans. One described them as 'a cloud of men, none of them wearing uniform, mounted on thin little horses of extraordinary lightness, which obeyed the rider's voice and the pressure of his knees, without the use of bridle or stirrups'[22]. Marmont organised another incursion in 1810 against the main Turkish raiding base at Izaćić, using four Grenzer and two French battalions supported by artillery. Napoleon was not impressed, but they succeeded in pacifying the Ottomans and gained the French prestige amongst the Grenzers.

In 1813, as the French position deteriorated after the retreat from Moscow, the Bosnians renewed their raiding. The situation was stabilised, but the

Grenzer units were less committed to fighting against the advancing British in Dalmatia. As elsewhere in the occupied lands, French economic and administrative reforms played second fiddle to military requirements, and the Grenzer were unhappy about the French failure to support the Serbian revolt. As Austria moved towards declaring war against France in 1813, revolts were encouraged, and units mutinied as Austrian forces advanced into Croatia. The invasion was led by General Radivojevic with six infantry battalions and six squadrons of cavalry, along with twelve thousand muskets to rearm the Grenzer.

Ali Pasha

We left Ali Pasha enjoying his gains after the Russo-Ottoman campaign against the French in the Ionian Islands. His control of the mainland ports pleased the government in Istanbul as it kept the Russians on the islands. Ali was also in favour as he had contributed to the armies that attempted to deal with Osman Pasvanoglu. In 1800, the Islands were formed into the Septinsular Republic, paying tribute to the Ottoman Empire but under the joint protection of the Russians and the Ottomans. Religious freedom was honoured, with no extra taxation or Muslim immigration. However, civil unrest gave the Russians an excuse to increase their garrison, effectively putting the Islands under Russian protection. Parga continued to resist Ali Pasha's attempts to take control of the port by getting Istanbul to appoint a governor for protection, an arrangement confirmed in the Peace of Amiens in 1802. Replacing Russian for French influence on Greek nationalism was little improvement for Ali or the Porte, although the Russians were less active and less willing to provide military supplies. The Reverend Hughes, a British traveller, was clear about Ali's intentions: 'As long as he lives he will exert all his energies to gain a footing in the Ionian Islands, and upon his death-bed he will bequeath these sentiments to a successor.'[23]

In these circumstances, Ali got approval to attack his old enemies, the Souliots, having failed to crush them back in 1792. The tiny republic of Souli was based in the mountains of Thesprotia, around fifty miles southwest of Ali Pasha's headquarters at Ioannina. It was a natural fortress with four main villages that could only be reached by one steep passage three miles long. As one English traveller somewhat excitedly described it, 'If the woods were gloomy and the mountains wild, the chasms were terrific and the magnificence awful'[24].

Souli (Author)

The villages housed some twelve thousand people, with all males conscripted and trained in warfare from the age of ten, and it was not unknown for women to take an active role in fighting. Souliots had become experts in guerrilla warfare and were renowned for their courage. As Lord Byron was to say:

> Oh! Who is more brave than a dark Suliote.
> In his snowy camese and his shaggy capote?
> To the wolf and the vulture he leaves his wild flock,
> And descends on the plain like a stream from the rock.

The last line references the Souliot practice of extorting tribute from around sixty villages in the plains below, some as far as seven hours' journey from Souli. While the Souliots can be romanticised, we should remember that they were as guilty of brigandage as any others in the region. Souli did have a sipahi timar (fief), Bekir Bey, who was based in Ioannina and went to collect his rents annually. Ali tried several times to buy the sipahi's rights, but he refused. So, Ali found a reason to imprison him, and when he still wouldn't sell, he hanged him. As a 19th-century historian of Souli puts it, that was a 'most efficacious expedient'![25]

Having learned from his past mistakes, Ali avoided a frontal assault on Souli and instead adopted a war of attrition. First, he blockaded Souli with a ring of forts and bribed some Souliots to join him. Then, with the support of neighbouring pashas, he assembled an army of around twenty thousand men. Attempts to buy the remaining Souliots out of their fortresses failed: 'You flatter yourself in vain, since our liberty is neither to be sold nor bought with all the treasure in the world, but with the blood and death of the last Suliote.'[26] In the autumn of 1803, the increasingly desperate and starving Souliots finally agreed to abandon their homeland—although a faction decided on death rather than capitulation, and blew up their arsenal as Ali's troops entered.

Around four thousand survivors went to Parga and the Ionian Islands, including seventeen hundred to Corfu, though some accounts have them being attacked by Ali's men. Women had also taken part in defence of the Souliot lands; Major Leake reported one wife saying, 'When Ali threatened to roast alive her son Foto, who was in his hands, she replied, that she was young, and could have other children, and that she would eat a bit of the roasted flesh rather than betray her country.' The story of a mass suicide of Souliot women became famous across Europe as the 'Dance of Zalongo'. There is a monument on the site today. The dance has been orchestrated by N. Skalkottas in *36 Greek Dances*:

> The fish cannot live on the land,
> Nor the flower on the sand,
> And the women of Suli
> Cannot live without freedom.

Many surviving male Souliots took service with the Russians and then the French in their Albanian Regiment. The British generally did not employ them; ironically, many returned to the mainland and joined Ali Pasha's army in 1820.

Russian propaganda encouraged the raids of Greek klephts, often described in nationalist literature as anti-Ottoman insurgents because of their later role in the Greek War of Independence. In this period, they were primarily brigands in the mountains who raided travellers and isolated settlers. Ali launched several campaigns against the klephts with mixed success, and some joined Ali's forces as *armatoli*, a form of Ottoman irregular. Both groups made alliances with the Ottomans and robbed Christians as much as

Muslims. Klephts operated in small bands led by captains including Antonis Katsantonis, Nikos Tsaras and Demitrios Palaeopolos.

The British sent Jack Morier as Consul General to Albania and the Morea in 1804. He was very impressed by Ali, both as a strong regional power and as a bulwark against foreign powers. Ali boasted to Morier that the French had offered Corfu if he would permit a landing on the coast to French forces based in Italy. Even so, Morier argued that a French invasion through Ali's territory was unlikely, given the harsh terrain and the absence of roads. This had the effect of downgrading Ali's importance to the British, who had already sent Captain (later Major) Leake as a military advisor. His role was to ensure that Ali's territory could be defended against a French attack, and strengthen him in his internal conflicts as Britain's best ally in the region. The Russian plenipotentiary, Count Mocenigo, was much more hostile to Ali, and this was reciprocated, making joint action between the allies difficult. Ali always viewed the Russians as the main threat.

The outbreak of war between the Russians and Ottomans in 1806 allowed Ali to occupy the ports of Butrint, Igoumenitsa and Vonitsa. However, Parga again resisted with the help of a Russian garrison. Ali prepared to attack Santa Maura (Lefkada), where many klephts and Souliots had been exiled, including Theodore Kolokotronis[27]. Ali had reopened diplomatic relations with the French after Austerlitz, who were now his neighbours in Dalmatia. He gained several French advisors, including an artillery expert, General Guillaume de Vaudoncourt. The three thousand defenders on Parga mainly were refugees from Ali's domains who had enlisted in a Russian light infantry regiment, supported by Russian troops and a French engineer in Russian service, Colonel Michaud. Commanded by Count Kapodistria, they fortified the narrow isthmus, the only approach to the island, and hired a fleet of boats to guard against a sea attack. Greek klephts on the mainland attacked Ali's villages as the garrison skirmished with Ali's forces.

Parga Castle (Author)

Events elsewhere once again frustrated Ali. Under the Treaty of Tilsit (July 1807), the Russians gave the Ionian Islands to France. French garrisons replaced the Russians, and diplomatic efforts by Ali to acquire the island and Parga were rebuffed by Napoleon. The French governor, General Berthier, created new regiments from Greek volunteers. Ali refused orders from the Porte to cooperate with the French. However, the British ambassador reported that they were secretly encouraging Ali.[28] Napoleon wanted to create a new line of communication from Cattaro to Corfu through Albania, which the Porte rejected. Ali had friends at court, suitably recompensed, that could intercede on his behalf.

Ali's aggressive actions had created a new unity amongst the klephts and armatoli, turning them into a confederacy that challenged the control of the mountain passes. Ali sent his son Mukhtar with four thousand troops to destroy them. Popular support for the confederacy had waned when they resorted to brigandage, and several leaders were betrayed and captured. They met a typically violent end at Ali's hands, with one having his bones crushed with a sledgehammer.

Having failed to win over the French, Ali shifted his attention back to the British, hoping to get them to invade the Islands on his behalf. Several effusive letters from Ali to the British in the National Archives reflect this. In one, after much flattery and regret over past misunderstandings, he asks for 'a squadron of four or five large ships which would be very useful for the necessary protection of the coast.'[29] Unsurprisingly, the reply ducked the question of ships that the British had no prospects of being able to allocate to such a task, even if they wanted to. Following the Ottoman-British peace treaty (January 1809), the British liaison officer at Ali's court, Major Leake, provided artillery and ammunition for use against the French. He was, however, authorised to hold back some of the artillery 'if it could be done without offence to Ali Pasha' for the Pasha of Scutari.

The British started to pick off the Ionian Islands one after another, encouraging desertions amongst the Greek troops in French service. This helped to convince Ali that the British were in the ascendency. The British were concerned about strengthening him against French and Russian efforts to dismember the Ottoman Empire. Meanwhile, the French supported a confederation of Ali's enemies, led by Ibrahim Pasha of Berat. Ali managed to defeat this threat with the help of six hundred Congreve rockets supplied by Leake, and extended his domains northwards to Durazzo. Given the erratic nature of these weapons, Wellington was not impressed. It would be interesting to know how Ali's troops fared with them.

The British interest in Ali was not solely as a military buffer against the French. They viewed the Albanian port of Durazzo (Durrës) as a convenient place to export corn, wool, timber and tobacco, and import British goods such as sugar, cloth and coffee. Leake's papers contain a detailed report on the suitability of Albanian timber for use by the Royal Navy[30]. Stronger relations with the British did not stop Ali from continuing to keep his options open with the French. He professed his loyalty to France in 1811 when the French consul to the region visited him for two weeks.

The Sultan was becoming increasingly concerned about Ali's growing power, including occupying Ochrid and Elbasan, and tried to weaken him by removing his sons, Mukhtar and Veli, from their pashaliks. However, this came to nothing as the war against Russia meant the Sultan needed their troops. Ali, worried about being arrested, did not go in person to the Danube in 1811, but he promised thirty thousand troops, with Mukhtar providing ten thousand and Veli twenty thousand. As we will see, the British replaced the Russians in the islands Ali coveted. He returned to the offensive against Berat, taking Argyrocastro and Delvino (in modern Albania).

This exposed the village of Gardiki to Ali's vengeance for the molestation of his mother and sister when he was a child. With a force of fifteen thousand men, Ali slaughtered much of the population and sold others into slavery. A stone memorial there includes the words, 'He has razed our unfortunate town to the ground, and ordered that it may remain a desert forever'. It did not pay to cross Ali Pasha, who used such displays to deter others, saying, 'When I consider this terrible slaughter, I am much grieved, and I desire that so great an evil shall never occur again: For which reason I give notice to all my neighbours that they must not molest my house but be obedient, in order that they may be happy.'[31]

In 1812, Ali had yet another crack at Parga and its French garrison, with a force of six thousand men supported by ships from Preveza. With the French garrison weakened by Napoleon's Russian campaign, the population shifted their allegiance to the British and rose in revolt on 22 March 1814. Captain Garland arrived with British troops diverted from the siege of Corfu and took possession. Ali was furious and complained to the British and the Sultan, who ignored him. He bombarded Lord Castlereagh at the Congress of Vienna on this point, receiving polite but evasive responses.[32] However, after our period, Ali finally got his way when the British traded Parga for Ottoman recognition of their occupation of the Ionian Islands. Ali had to pay £150,000 for the privilege, and most of the Pargians left for Corfu, even disinterring the bones of their ancestors.

The Napoleonic Wars may have ended in 1815. Still, Ali Pasha played an important role in the region, including the Greek War of Independence, for which he is given insufficient credit. Ali may have been a rogue, but he kept a turbulent region under control, a skill the Porte would later need.

Western visitors were fascinated by Ali Pasha, sometimes describing the region as an oriental fantasy land. However, official British papers describing his chaotic administration called him the 'most monstrous tyrant'. Richard Davenport (who wrote a biography of Ali[33]) put it bluntly: 'I have never followed any road previously travelled by Ali Pasha without seeing some newly filled up grave, or some wretches hanging on trees. His footsteps are stained with blood.' The French did not have any better view of Ali. Their consul Pouqueville wrote, 'His guard is composed of assassins; his pages are depraved children of victims of his ferocity; his emissaries, blackguardly Vlachs, ready to commit any crime, and his confidential agents poisoners who glory in their wickedness.'[34] Many of these travelogues have been criticised as orientalist literature, voyeuristic, manipulated and distorted; others disagree, arguing that they can be informative[35].

Not everyone was so critical of Ali, and other travellers noted the relative security in the lands he controlled. The British consul, Morier, argued that the suppression of the Souliots benefitted peace in the region, and the British continued to support Ali pragmatically as the best defence against the French in the region. Noel Malcolm argues that Ali's primary goal was to maintain his territory and its resources. In the decentralised Ottoman empire of the period, he did not need independence to achieve that, although something similar to the autonomous Barbary States might be desirable. The Napoleonic Wars destabilised the region, and Ali played a clever game seeking to benefit from the changes. Malcolm concludes, 'His own power had been great while it had lasted, however; and it is testimony to his extraordinary skill that he sustained it, in one of the most internationally contested areas of the Ottoman Empire, through all the twists and turns of a major European war.'[36]

A collection of Ali Pasha's weapons in Ioannina (Author)

CHAPTER FOUR

FRENCH EXPANSION—1802-09

In June 1802, the Ottomans signed the Treaty of Paris, restoring French-Ottoman relations to their positive state before Napoleon invaded Egypt. The consulate had dispatched General Sébastiani to the Levant, where he attempted to mediate between the Mamelukes and Porte. Horace François Bastien Sébastiani was a Corsican who joined the revolutionary army before supporting Napoleon in the Brumaire coup (he was probably a distant relative). He was Napoleon's Middle East expert who was sent on various military and diplomatic expeditions in the region. He was promoted to general of division after Austerlitz, where he was wounded. He later served with little distinction in the Peninsular War, and in the Russian campaign he was the first French commander to enter Moscow. He survived supporting Napoleon during the Hundred Days and had a mixed political career, being briefly considered for premier in the 1830s. He was probably a better politician than a soldier, even though he was made a Marshal of France in 1840.

Horace Sébastiani, with the Hagia Sophia in the background

While in the Levant, he devised a plan to reestablish French control over Egypt and parts of the Ottoman Empire. The report was published by *Le Moniteur Universel* on 30 January 1803, threatening British and Russian interests, adding to the dispute over Malta and justifying British troops remaining there while France held designs to invade Egypt. Fortunately, the Ottomans did not appear to take this initiative seriously. This is just as well because Sébastiani later became the French ambassador to the Porte.

Britain and France had been preparing for a new conflict, raising new troops and ships. The *casus belli* was ostensibly the British occupation of Malta, and after a tirade by Napoleon against the British ambassador, Britain declared war on France on 16 May 1803. This was somewhat earlier than Napoleon had planned, and he imposed an embargo on British goods, a precursor to the later continental blockade. This became the War of the Third Coalition when Austria and Russia declared war on France.

For the Austrians, Napoleon's actions in Germany, including the occupation of Hanover and effective control over Bavaria and Wurttemberg, pushed them to fight. Napoleon also seized the Adriatic ports of Ancona, Brindisi and Otranto, which threatened Austrian interests. Archduke Charles was against the war, pointing to the disparity between French and Austrian armies (421

French infantry battalions as against 240 Austrian), a poor state of preparedness, and the unreliability of Russia as an ally. However, the Emperor listened to others (mainly General Mack), and a deal was signed with the Russians on 6 November 1804 to provide one hundred and fifteen thousand troops.

Austria formally joined the Third Coalition in August 1805. The Prussians were bought off when Napoleon offered them Hanover. The disastrous 1805 campaign in central Europe is outside the scope of this book, but the capitulation of sixty thousand Austrian troops at Ulm (20 October) was the end of General Mack. Archduke Charles held General Massena's French army in Italy at the Battle of Caldiero (29-31 October), but as Napoleon advanced and occupied Vienna, he withdrew into Hungary. The campaign reached its climax on 2 December at the Battle of Austerlitz, one of Napoleon's greatest victories.

Elsewhere, Spain joined the war in December 1804 after Royal Navy frigates captured the bullion convoy from America that would have been used to pay the treaty subsidy to France. The four British frigate captains did very well out of the naval action, receiving £15,000 (around £1.1 million today) in prize money[1]. British domination of the seas was complete following the Battle of Trafalgar on 21 October 1805.

Meanwhile, the Ionian Islands fell into internal disarray, and British and Russian troops occasionally intervened. Black Sea trade boomed during this period, with Odessa (Odesa) growing in importance for grain exports. The Russians believed a presence in the Mediterranean was essential to maintain the security of this trade. So, in 1804, a Russian squadron of three frigates brought Russian troops to strengthen the garrison of the Ionian Islands, largely made up of local militia. Several further detachments were sent throughout 1804, increasing the Russian force in the islands to over thirteen thousand soldiers. Ships came and went, but to avoid weakening the Black Sea Fleet, a squadron was dispatched from the Baltic on 24 October under Captain-Commodore Aleksey Samuilovich Greig, with *Sv. Elena* (74), *Retvizan* (64), *Venus* (50) and *Avtroil* (32) arriving at Corfu on 23 January 1805. The Russians also strengthened their position across the Balkans by appointing consuls in key towns.

Greig was one of several Russian officers of Scottish descent. He was born in the Russian naval base of Kronstadt in 1775. His father, who had been born in Inverkeithing, was one of several Royal Navy officers sent to assist the Russian navy, and had risen to the rank of Russian admiral. Alexsey studied at the Royal High School, Edinburgh, before starting his naval career in the

British Royal Navy. He served in East India and Europe from 1785 to 1796, including as a volunteer on board HMS *Culloden*, under Captain (later Rear-Admiral and First Naval Lord) Thomas Troubridge. He then returned to Russia and took part in the Mediterranean campaigns. In 1816 Greig became Commander of the Black Sea Fleet, a post he held for seventeen years. He was also the Military Governor of Sevastopol and Nikolayev (Mykolaiv), introducing many reforms; the grateful citizens of Nikolayev erected a statue to his memory in 1873.

Admiral Aleksey Samuilovich Greig

Italy

One of the first actions in the war was in the Adriatic when Napoleon ordered General Gouvion St Cyr to advance along the Adriatic coast into Neapolitan territory. King Ferdinand of Naples, recognising the threat, agreed to stay neutral (Treaty of Naples, October 1805), and St Cyr withdrew on 21 September 1805. However, the French army had always held onto the strategic Adriatic ports of Taranto, Bari, and Brindisi with a fourteen-thousand-strong garrison, again on the basis that the British had not abandoned Malta. Ferdinand quickly allowed British and Russian troops back, effectively joining the Third Coalition. General Craig brought seventy-five hundred British troops from Malta, while General Maurice Lacy (of Irish descent) brought thirteen thousand Russian troops from Corfu, although the numbers in both commands may have been smaller.

Craig and Lacy planned to attack northern Italy, but found the notional twenty-two-thousand-strong Neapolitan Army totally unprepared for war. They therefore deployed defensively on the frontier with the British behind the Garigliano River, the Russians on their right in the Apennine Mountains, and a small Neapolitan force under General Roger de Damas on the Adriatic coast. Conscription marginally increased the Neapolitan Army, and an additional six thousand Russian troops were promised. However, the Austro-Russian defeat at Austerlitz (2 December 1805) ended the Third Coalition, and Lacy was ordered to withdraw his depleted troops from Italy to Corfu. Craig withdrew the British forces to Sicily.

After a French army led by Massena invaded Naples in February 1806, King Ferdinand retreated to Sicily. Napoleon's brother Joseph was appointed King of the Two Sicilies in Naples. Only the presence of British troops and a guerrilla war in the Calabrian mountains kept Joseph from invading Sicily. Craig went home ill and was replaced by General Sir John Stuart, while Admiral Sydney Smith commanded the naval forces. The British government was considering attacks on the new French bases in the Adriatic when Craig arrived home and persuaded ministers to focus on defending Sicily. Stuart rejected several impractical schemes suggested by Smith and then landed his army of sixty-four hundred troops on the mainland. He was attacked by the French General Reynier at Maida on 3 July 1806, and after defeating him, he mopped up French garrisons on the coast before returning to Sicily. The battle is at least remembered in London, as Maida Vale is named after it.

The Russians agreed to a defensive treaty with the Ottomans in September 1805, which allowed Russian ships to pass through the Straits into the Mediterranean. The treaty was aimed at France and provided for military help totalling six ships of the line and four frigates together with ten thousand infantry and twenty thousand cavalry. Secret clauses in the treaty allowed the Russian troops to be transported to their garrison in the Ionian Islands through the Straits. Despite this, the treaty fell short of Russian expectations. The Ottomans rejected Russian proposals to deploy ten to fifteen thousand troops in the Danubian principalities and transfer Parga to Russia. Proposed equal rights for the Sultan's Christian subjects, and the Tsar's right to intervene on their behalf, fared no better. The Russian ambassador in Istanbul wrote to the Tsar, 'It is a sharp pain, Sire, a genuine anxiety that I feel when thinking that I am presenting to you a document which does not comply entirely with your wishes, but over which, I have to respectfully reassure your majesty, I didn't have the control required to provide a better shape.'[2] Russian troops in the Caucasus, capturing the port of Anaklia, did not help the negotiations, even though the troops subsequently withdrew. The well-resourced French embassy in Istanbul was wrong-footed by the treaty, although even this limited rapprochement between the Russians and Ottomans did not last long. Napoleon's humiliation of the Austrians at Ulm and Austerlitz returned the Porte to its previous French sympathies. Napoleon started to pressure the Ottomans to close the Straits to Russian ships.

The Treaty of Pressburg (26 December 1805) brought the War of the Third Coalition to an end for the Austrians, who handed Venetia, Dalmatia, Istria and the Bay of Cattaro to France. This brought Napoleonic France to the borders of the Ottoman Empire. The new provinces were initially absorbed into the Kingdom of Italy, which had been created on 17 March 1805. Napoleon was crowned King in May, but he was represented by the Viceroy, later his designated heir, Eugène de Beauharnais. Not that Napoleon believed in delegating much to his stepson, saying, 'Your system of government is simple: the emperor wills it to be thus.' Initially, the French took a pragmatic view toward reforming the new provinces. Napoleon appointed the Italian intellectual Vincenzo Dandolo to govern Dalmatia between 1807 and 1809. He brought administrative reforms and urban improvements, but thought the wholesale imposition of the Napoleonic legal system was too complex.

The war of the Fourth Coalition broke out in October 1806. As Austria was not engaged, the war only had the effect of drawing French forces north to the focus of the war in Prussia. Even that was short-lived following Napoleon's victories at Jena/Auerstadt, which knocked Prussia out of the war.

Dalmatian Campaign of 1806

The Russian squadrons in the Adriatic could come from the Black Sea Fleet only when Russia was at peace with the Ottomans, as access was through the Straits. This meant that reinforcements otherwise had to come from the Baltic, which also had better ships. In 1805 Vice-Admiral Dmitriy Nikolayevich Senyavin was appointed to command naval and land forces in the Mediterranean[3]. Senyavin came from a naval family and graduated from the

Naval Cadet Corps in 1780. He took part in an expedition to Portugal, joined the Black Sea Fleet upon its formation in 1783, and helped construct the naval base in Sevastopol. During the Russo-Turkish War (1787-92), he was present at the battles of Fidonisi and Ochakov and distinguished himself in command of *Navarchia* during the Battle of Caliacria. During Ushakov's Mediterranean expedition of 1798-1800, Senyavin commanded *Svyatoy Pyotr* (72). In 1804, he was promoted to rear admiral and commanded the port in Reval.

Vice-Admiral Dmitriy Nikolayevich Senyavin

Senyavin's squadron consisted of his flagship, *Yaroslav* (74); *Moskva* (74), *Svyatoy Pyotr* (74), *Selafail* (74), *Uriil* (84), the frigate *Kildyuin* (32) and two brigs. By the standards of the naval war in the Adriatic, these were large ships, unlike the frigates and brigs that the British and French generally deployed in the region. They joined the Russian squadron already in the Adriatic, commanded by Captain-Commodore Greig, who would be promoted to Rear Admiral on 8 January 1806. Greig's squadron comprised five ships of the line: *Retvizan* (64), *Svyataya Yelena* (74), *Svyataya Paraskeva* (74), *Aziya* (74), and

Svyatoy (used as a troop transport), along with four frigates, six corvettes, and six brigs.

It was this fleet that allowed the Russians to intervene on the mainland. The Montenegrins and the Bokez (citizens of the Bay of Cattaro (Kotor)) were sympathetic to Russia, and through the Russian consul in Montenegro (Stefan Sankovskiy) they encouraged Senyavin to occupy Cattaro and the eight forts in the bay when the Austrians were supposed to hand it over to the French in 1806. The weight of gunfire from the large Russian ships was often sufficient to persuade French garrisons to capitulate. A Russian squadron under Captain Baillie, consisting of three ships of the line (*Aziya*, *Svyataya Yelena* and *Yaroslav*) with two frigates and smaller vessels, bombarded Curzola (Korcula) port, taking less than thirty minutes to disable the town's guns. Landing parties of sailors and marines took other garrisons. Russian ships also blockaded ports and captured French merchant ships as prizes. In May 1806, French General Molitor was travelling from Venice to Trieste when his merchant ship was intercepted. He managed to persuade the Russian captain that he was an Austrian merchant. The fact that he carried papers to support this claim indicates that this was not a one-off precaution.

A further squadron of Russian ships from the Baltic arrived at Corfu. This included *Silny* (74), *Rafail* (84), *Moshchnyy* (74), *Tvyordyy* (84), *Skoryy* (64), the frigate *Lyogkiy* (44), the sloop *Shpitsbergen* (32), the corvette *Flora* (24) and the cutter *Strela* (18). In Corfu, General Lacy was replaced by Admiral Senyavin in command of land and sea forces; in addition to taking over Cattaro (Kotor), he also seized the Island of Lissa (Vis). The Russians garrisoned Cattaro and Castelnuovo with two battalions of the Vitebsk Regiment, commanded by Major-General Musin-Pushkin. The Bay of Cattaro is a stunning natural harbour with several small towns, which attracted the Venetians and then the Austrians, and it linked well with Russian support for Montenegro.

Bay of Kotor (Author)

The Ottomans generally ignored the small mountainous state, which had maintained its autonomy despite the attentions of Ottoman governors, under the rule of its Prince-Bishop Peter I. Tsar Paul recognised their independence and gave them a Russian subsidy of three thousand rubles in 1799. Alexander was briefly persuaded to abandon Peter I, but the Russian consul resolved the differences in 1803. The French also made overtures to the Montenegrins, but as Slavs and Orthodox Christians, they were more inclined to the Russians. Russian officers describe Montenegrin boys firing off pistols and shouting, 'Long live our Tsar Alexander; may the infidel perish!' Others were full of praise for the hospitality they received when exploring the countryside, although the Montenegrin practice of firing welcoming gunshots that 'whistle past one's ears' could be disconcerting![4] The Russians recognised the strategic merits of Cattaro and got there well before the French. Senyavin used his initiative to intervene, arguing that the Treaty of Pressburg did not apply to Russia. He later explained to the Tsar that Cattaro had four hundred merchant ships, five thousand seamen, and twelve thousand citizens under arms, which was probably an exaggeration[5].

The French forces led by General Molitor marched into Dalmatia in 1806. Molitor joined the army during the revolutionary wars as a captain of militia and fought in Switzerland under Massena. He was promoted to general of division in 1801. He served in all the coalition wars, other than the Russian campaign. He was made a marshal only after the restoration. Molitor was reinforced with a division under General Lauriston as they moved down the coast. Lauriston, who was born in French India, was of Scottish descent (Lauriston Castle is near Edinburgh). He was an artillery officer who served in the revolutionary wars and became an aide-de-camp to Napoleon in 1800. He was promoted to general of division in 1805 and, after this campaign, became the governor of Venice. He served in the 1809 and 1812 campaigns before being captured at Leipzig in 1813. He also made Marshal of France after the restoration.

In the way of the French was the Republic of Ragusa (Dubrovnik), which included the city and the mainland coast from Neum to the Prevlaka peninsula, the Pelješac peninsula, and the islands of Lastovo and Mljet. Four thousand people lived in the city, and another thirty-one thousand in the wider state territory. It was a republic ruled by twenty-four noble families, no more than one hundred people in total, who wore black robes and served in a Venetian-style Senate. The peasants worked as serfs (*kmets*), with many young men escaping to serve at sea. An Austrian spy noted, 'The patricians view their subordinates as slaves, and everyone outside their class as inferior'[6]. Ragusa's trading empire was being challenged, but with 190 trading vessels, its merchant fleet was larger than those of Venice or Prussia. There were four hundred shipowners employing about twenty-two hundred sailors, and they could build fourteen types of vessels in their twelve shipyards.

Fortifications of Ragusa (Author)

The Republic was a firmly Catholic enclave in an Orthodox and Muslim hinterland and had generally poor relations with Russia. While it sought to exploit its impoverished hinterland, it lived in fear and loathing of the people of the Dinaric Alps around it. General Bertrand, a French military commandant of Ragusa, was impressed by its intellectual life and described it as 'a city remarkable for its urbanity...situated amid barbarism.'[7] The Peace of Loeben had transformed Austria from a distant and usually benevolent power into the Republic's neighbour. They were only separated by the two Ottoman buffer zones of Klek and Sutorina. The Republic subsequently resisted Austrian claims to hegemony and negotiated a trade deal with France. Enlightenment ideas began to take hold in the city, despite the banning of radical books, including a Patriotic Society to discuss reform. These developments alarmed Austria, which indicated it had intercepted letters from Jacobins in the city to their allies in Venice, although without providing evidence[8]. Tax increases on the peasants had resulted in the Konavle Revolt of 1799, ironically primarily to pay for French extortion. This led to the peasants calling on the Austrians for protection.

On 15 March 1806, a Russian squadron under Captain Henry Baillie started a blockade of the port, capturing twenty-six Ragusan merchant ships. He then grabbed the island of Curzola (Korcula), which dominated the sea route to Ragusa from the north. The Republic was desperate to stay neutral and rejected an offer to pay off the French, pointing to the Russian threat to devastate their territory if they allowed the French through. They could have asked the Russian squadron for aid, but the prospect of an influx of Slavs caused them to favour the French. Lauriston demanded that his troops be allowed to rest and be supplied, but when they entered the city on 27 May, they seized control. The Republic was subsequently abolished and incorporated into the Kingdom of Italy (1808).

On 3 June, Russian marines seized the town of Ragusa-Vecchia south of the city, supported by a Russian invasion force of seventeen hundred men under Major General Viazemsky, and twenty-five hundred Montenegrins under Peter I. The French built a series of redoubts south of the city on the Bergatto Heights, garrisoned by French and Ragusan troops. On 17 June, Viazemsky's force managed to scale the heights and captured nineteen guns, forcing Lauriston back to the city walls. Lauriston was then blockaded by the Russians in Ragusa. At the same time, they bombarded the city, and local Slavs looted the surrounding area. On 18 June, a landing party of six hundred marines and sailors supported by a company of *jagers* landed on the island of San Marco, situated off the coast from the city walls. The well-entrenched French troops fought off several assaults on the fortifications, and the Russians withdrew. The Russians then cut off the water supply and dragged ships' guns to the mountains above the city. An estimated eighteen hundred to three thousand projectiles rained upon the inhabitants during the siege. The Russian fleet could also interdict French supply columns coming down the Dalmatian coast, so the French were forced to put convoys on donkeys and take them over the mountains. Later they built a road using forced local labour, known as 'Napoleon's Road'. Despite the blockade, the city was well supplied with food, and Lauriston refused calls to surrender. Instead, he launched several sorties on the Russian and Montenegrin lines.

Molitor reached Ragusa on 5 July with three thousand (other sources say fifteen hundred) French reinforcements, which he took into Ottoman territory and flanked the Russian positions. The Montenegrins initially held their position, but many had started to drift home with their plunder. Their looting included stripping houses of moveable property and even digging up bodies to remove any iron[9]. The Russians organised an orderly withdrawal with the 13th Jagers detached as a fighting rearguard. The fleet removed the Russian forces under cover of their guns, abandoning all Ragusan territory by 8 July.

Senyavin received contradictory instructions from Tsar Alexander, which reflected the state of Russian-Austrian negotiations. Senyavin believed that he had a better grasp of the local situation, which is another example of how local commanders in the Adriatic had much more scope for independent action.

In August, Marshal Marmont arrived at Ragusa with three infantry divisions of the Army of Dalmatia, bringing the French forces to over ten thousand men. The Russians reinforced their land forces in the Bay of Cattaro from Corfu (two battalions of the Kolyvan and Kozlov regiments and four companies from the Vitebsk Regiment), and the Montenegrins rejoined the fight in defence of their territory. The French built batteries on the Cape of Ostro, which commands one side of the entrance to the Bay of Cattaro. However, an attack by Russian and Montenegrin troops on 25 September, supported by gunfire from the fleet, forced them to abandon the position. A French counterattack pushed the Russians and Montenegrins back to Castelnuovo (Herceg Novi); there, after a fierce battle on 1 October, the French forced the defenders back into the town. Three hundred fifty Russians and four hundred Montenegrins were killed, and the French lost twenty-five dead and one hundred and thirty injured. However, without heavy artillery and naval support, Marmont could not dislodge the defenders, and he withdrew to Ragusa, pursued by the Montenegrins. Russian naval support was again crucial to the defence. Nevertheless, the French claimed they were satisfied with the outcome. Marmont said, 'I had attained my goal and shown the barbarian peoples my superiority over the Russians.' He was subsequently appointed Duke of Ragusa by Napoleon.

Fortress at Castelnuovo (Herceg Novi) (Author)

By October, significant French forces had been withdrawn to central Europe for the Prussian campaign, leaving small scattered garrisons in Dalmatia. The Russians took advantage with a new offensive that recaptured Curzola (Korcula) on 12 December, defended by the French 81st Regiment, using three ships of the line (*Selafail*, *Svyataya Yelena* and *Yaroslav*) with the 14th Jagers and Montenegrin troops. In December, they added the islands of Hvar and Brac, which allowed the Russians to control access to Spalato (Split). Militarily this led to a stalemate, with the French unable to dislodge the Russians and their allies without committing large numbers of troops needed elsewhere and bringing a fleet into the Adriatic. The Montenegrins gained access to the sea and benefitted economically from the decline of Ragusa. Meanwhile, Tsar Alexander was minded to seek a peace agreement with France, and sent an envoy to Paris in May 1806. The envoy agreed to a preliminary treaty (Oubril Treaty 20 July 1806) that provided for a Russian withdrawal from the Ionian Islands and the Adriatic. Still, at this time, these terms went too far for Alexander.

Naval attack on Istanbul

French diplomacy in Istanbul had limited success before 1806. Napoleon had a direct diplomatic style, which probably grated with the Porte. One such letter said, 'Are you blind to your own interests? If Russia has an army at Corfu, do you believe it is directed at me? Your dynasty is about to descend into the night of oblivion.'[10] However, other French diplomats were subtler, and their agents and consuls across the Balkans were building an anti-Russian coalition. In July 1806, Sébastiani, who we met earlier as Napoleon's ambassador to the Levant, was sent as the new French ambassador to the Porte with explicit instructions to build a French-Ottoman-Persian alliance against Russia, including the closure of the Bosporus to Russian ships. Like the British, the French had come around to the view that the Ottoman Empire had to be propped up. He later met Kutuzov and described the Sultan's realm as an 'empire with a rotten core destined to fall apart.'[11] Sébastiani brought a military mission that included artillery Colonel Foy, the engineer Major Haxo, and three hundred gunners. This was a role Napoleon had once considered for himself[12]. Instead of partitioning the Ottoman Empire, Napoleon now favoured its consolidation. The defeat of the Russians at Austerlitz, coupled with Senyavin's actions in the Adriatic, paved the way for Sébastiani. In September, the Porte requested the cessation of Russian military transit through the Straits, which would cut off Senyavin from the Russian Black Sea Fleet.

To 'encourage' the Turks not to give in to Napoleon's pressure, the Royal Navy's Mediterranean fleet under Admiral Collingwood decided on a bit of gunboat diplomacy. Collingwood had served with Nelson in several campaigns since they first met in 1777 and was a captain at the naval battles of the Glorious First of June and Cape St Vincent. Promoted to admiral, he commanded the first line of ships to breach the Spanish line at Trafalgar and commanded the fleet after Nelson's death. Collingwood despatched Rear Admiral Thomas Louis with three ships of the line, a frigate and a sloop to Istanbul in November 1806. This force was reinforced with five more ships under Vice Admiral Duckworth, to make eight ships of the line, two frigates, and two sloops. However, Napoleon's pressure finally paid off; the Sultan secretly declared war on Russia on 16 December 1806, forcing the British ambassador to flee before being arrested.

The French under Sébastiani were strengthening the Ottoman gun batteries, and contrary winds held up Duckworth. On 19 February 1807, Duckworth entered the Straits, defeating a Turkish 64-gun ship and putting landing parties ashore to neutralise Ottoman artillery positions. The weather turned again when he was eight miles from Istanbul, just out of range of the city and the Ottoman fleet. With no prospect of being able to fire on the city and no army to put ashore, Duckworth decided to get back out of the Straits before the Ottoman artillery in the Dardanelles became too strong. He turned around on 29 February but still had to run past the huge Ottoman guns at the Dardanelles for what one sailor on board called 'another game of marbles.' Lieutenant Crawford, on board the flagship, described the marble and granite shot: 'I watched this monster-shot almost from the cannon's mouth till it struck the ship.... The whole scene on shore resembled the bursting of some mountain's side, which vomits forth in fire and smoke fragments of rock and iron.'[13] The flagship was struck by a marble shot weighing 500 pounds, and *Windsor Castle* by one that weighed 850 pounds and was over seven feet in circumference. By the time it sailed clear, the fleet had lost 29 killed and 138 wounded. Another week and the Dardanelles might have been impassable.

Kilitbahir Castle defended the Dardanelles (Author)

As Duckworth recovered at Tenedos island, Admiral Senyavin arrived with his eight ships and two thousand troops and asked for Duckworth's support in returning to Istanbul. Duckworth declined, arguing that two thousand men were insufficient to clear the shore defences, so Senyavin decided on a blockade. This caused food riots in the city and contributed to the overthrow of Sultan Selim III. The Turkish fleet under Seyit Ali made two sallies against the Russians, including landing troops on Tenedos. At the Battle of Athos (1-2 July), the Russians defeated the Turkish fleet using tactics similar to Nelson's at Trafalgar, splitting the Ottoman line and gaining local superiority. Only twelve of the twenty Ottoman ships returned safely to Istanbul—not one Russian ship was lost. The Black Sea Fleet also successfully attacked Ottoman positions at the entrance to the Sea of Azov, but an attack on Trebizond failed.

However, as our story often shows, events elsewhere intervened. Napoleon defeated the Russians at Friedland (14 June 1807), leading to an armistice on 12 August. The subsequent Treaty of Tilsit resulted in Russia abandoning much of its Adriatic possessions. Alexander was never an enthusiastic supporter of the war against France or the Adriatic strategy, and the conflict against the Ottomans confirmed the need for a new strategy. Admiral Senyavin's fleet was already suffering from a lack of funds and supplies, which were in part caused by communication challenges. Tilsit meant he was stranded in the Mediterranean without a base. He could not go back through the Straits, so he sent the troops home via Trieste and Austria, scuttled or sold some ships, and sailed the rest back towards the Baltic. He was blockaded by the British in Lisbon, and only two ships made it home in 1813. It was a tragic end for one of Russia's finest fleets that had operated successfully in the Adriatic. Admiral Senyavin fell out of favour on his return to St Petersburg and was posted to Reval. He resigned on 3 May 1813 and languished on half-pay until he was rehabilitated by Tsar Nicholas I in 1825.

Russo-Turkish War 1806-09

The Russo-Turkish War on land also was not going well for the Ottomans. In October 1806, the Russian Army of Dniester under General Michelson crossed the Dniester River and moved to occupy Bessarabia, Moldavia and Wallachia. However, he lost his 1st Corps (two divisions), diverted to central Europe as a consequence of Napoleon destroying the Prussian army at Jena. Still, thirty thousand men proved enough to capture most of the territories, with only Ismail, Braila, and Giurgiu left in Ottoman hands.

In 1807 the Porte mobilised from across the empire. The main army under Grand Vizier Ibrahim Hilmi Pasha gathered at Adrianople, and the Pasha of Bosnia sent twenty thousand troops to Vidin. The Russian army, now organised into three corps, was ordered to defend the Danube River line. This enabled Michelson to besiege Ismail, although Voinov's subsidiary attack on Kubya was halted. The Ottoman cavalry under Pehlivan dispersed the Cossacks, but the Russian infantry squares fought them off—a pattern which would often be repeated in the Russo-Turkish Wars of this period. The Ottomans launched several unsuccessful attacks on Russian forces shielding the advance on Ismail with actions at Turbat and Giurgiu on 17-18 March. Pehlivan was still able to reinforce Ismail and made several sorties.

By April, the Grand Vizier had reached the Danube with twenty-five thousand infantry, fifteen thousand cavalry and fifty guns. However, a janissary rebellion in Istanbul forced Sultan Selim III to resign, and the advance halted, awaiting instructions. The new Sultan Mustafa instructed that the offensive was to continue. The Ottomans crossed the Danube at Silistra and advanced on Bucharest to cut off the Russian siege of Ismail. Miloradovich's corps went with seven thousand men towards one of the Turkish columns commanded by Ali Pasha at Obilesti. On 19 June, Ali made several attacks on the Russian left flank, but the Russian squares fought them off, inflicting around three thousand casualties. Ali retreated toward the main army, and the Grand Vizier decided to pull back over the Danube. The victory at Obilesti, although overshadowed by the defeat at Friedland on 14 June, stopped the Turkish offensive, saved Bucharest, and gave the local population confidence in the Russian army.

The Peace of Tilsit included a provision that Napoleon was to mediate an armistice between the Russians and the Ottomans. However, the Tsar was not happy with two of the clauses in the armistice, and the Ottomans breached the conditions that their troops would not occupy towns abandoned by the Russians. Disputes over the terms of the armistice went on for several months. This allowed the reformist Mustafa Beyraktar, who we met earlier with Osman Pasvanoglu on the Danube, to intervene in Constantinople by marching a fifteen-thousand-strong army to the city, deposing Sultan Mustafa. He became the new Grand Vizier under Sultan Mahmud on 28 July 1808.

Peace with the French freed up Russian troops from central Europe for service in the Balkans, bringing the force up to eighty thousand men. The Russians also sent five infantry battalions and a Cossack regiment to the Serbs. The elderly Prince Prozorovsky was appointed to command the Moldavian

Army with General Kutuzov as his deputy. Mikhail Kutuzov is probably the best-known Russian general of the period, becoming commander in chief during the 1812 campaign. A career soldier, he served under Suvorov and was wounded in the Russo-Turkish War of 1768-1774. After travelling to Prussia and London, he returned to serve again with Suvorov in Crimea, becoming a Major General, and winning distinction in the 1787-1792 Russo-Turkish War. Tsar Alexander disastrously ignored his advice at Austerlitz, and he organised the army's retreat back to Russia.

Field-Marshal Mikhail Kutuzov (Gatchina museum preserve, public domain)

Prozorovsky and Kutuzov trained the Russian army to fight in two large squares (mobile redoubts) with cavalry in between. Given the chaos in the Ottoman Empire, Prozorovsky sought to provoke the Ottoman forces, writing, 'I used every means to provoke the Turks to attack either our troops or the Serbs, but all my attempts were futile'[14]. Napoleon then effectively sold out the Ottomans, making a deal with Alexander that gave him free rein in Spain in return for Russia's acquisition of Bessarabia, Moldavia and Wallachia (Congress of Erfurt, 14 October 1808). The Russians made an offer of peace based on the scope of the deal with Napoleon, but the Ottomans were again in chaos after another janissary rebellion resulted in the death of the Grand Vizier.

In 1809, the Russian position hardened when the British sought to make peace with the Ottomans after the latter had been abandoned by Napoleon.

This resulted in the Anglo-Ottoman Treaty of the Dardanelles on 5 January 1809. The treaty included secret articles establishing a defensive alliance between the Ottomans and Britain, although the Porte had no obligation to fight the French. When hostilities opened in April, both sides had similar-sized armies. The Ottomans had forty thousand men in garrisons along the Danube and a further forty thousand deployed between Adrianople and the Danube, commanded by the new Grand Vizier Yussuf Pasha. The Pashas of Bosnia and Nis were ordered to subdue the Serbs. The Russians moved to capture Giurgiu, with five columns commanded by Miloradovich attacking the entrenchments. Ottoman reinforcements and the local population rallied to the defences, and the Russians were forced to withdraw.

Meanwhile, Prozorovsky and Kutuzov marched on Braila with three corps. The first assault with eight thousand men fell into confusion after fierce fighting and casualties from friendly fire. After nearly five thousand casualties, the remaining Russian forces withdrew. After these failures, Alexander directed that the Danube fortresses be covered with detachments while the main army crossed the Danube and marched on Istanbul. He relied on the Ottoman Empire's internal problems to deliver victory before the British could provide significant assistance to the Porte. Prozorovsky was concerned about being attacked by the Austrians in his rear and an Anglo-Ottoman landing on the Black Sea coast. Alexander dismissed these concerns but agreed to Prozorovsky's request that Kutuzov, with whom he had fallen out, should leave the army, and be replaced by Prince Bagration.

The main army was divided in two, one to cross the Danube and the other to cover Wallachia. Prozorovsky led forty-one battalions and fifty squadrons with fifty-eight guns, as well as ten Cossack regiments organised into four corps, which crossed the Danube in July after building a bridge covered by batteries and gunboats. However, Prozorovsky fell ill and died on 18 August, leaving Prince Bagration to take command. Bagration supported the offensive strategy but needed to secure a crossing point by taking Girsov and Macin. The Russian bombardment of Macin blew up a gunpowder magazine, leaving the Ottoman forces in confusion. For the first time in this campaign, they agreed to an unconditional capitulation. Girsov also fell after a two-day bombardment which allowed the army to build a bridge across the Danube in addition to the ferry. Bagration divided his army of twenty-five thousand men (thirty-one battalions, forty-five squadrons, fifty-nine guns, and twelve Cossack regiments) into three corps: 1st Corps (Miloradovich), 2nd Corps (Platov), and 3rd Corps (Markov). The Grand Vizier threatened a counterattack from Giurgiu towards Bucharest to draw off the Russian advance. Count Langeron preempted this advance by taking a force of six thousand men from Bucharest towards Giurgiu. He met and defeated an Ottoman force under Bosnak Agha at Frasin on 10 September.

This allowed Prince Bagration to resume his advance towards a force of fifteen thousand men under Hozrev Mehmet Pasha that was blocking the Russian passage towards Silistra at Rassevat. Bagration combined his forces and attacked on 14 September by bombarding the camp while advancing in squares. Hozrev ordered a withdrawal, but his troops were caught, primarily by Cossacks, with heavy casualties, estimated at over four thousand with a further one thousand captured. One hundred thirty colours were also taken, including that of the Grand Vizier. There were promotions to full general for Miloradovich and Platov and the Order of St Andrew for Bagration. He also received fifty thousand rubles, while the rank and file received one ruble each—such was the lot of the ordinary Russian soldier!

The victory at Rassevat led to the capitulation of Ismail, while Bagration went on to besiege Silistra. The fortress was vigorously defended with a wide moat, 130 guns, and a garrison of 11,000 men commanded by Ilak Oglu. Bagration moved his batteries closer to the fortress, and along with gunboats on the Danube, he began a bombardment. There were frequent sorties, and the Grand Vizier moved forces towards the town to harass the Russian lines of communication. Napoleon had advised the Ottomans to avoid pitched battles and focus on a war of attrition. Alexander urged Bagration to press on with the offensive and defeat the Grand Vizier's army, because he was concerned that the conclusion of the French and Austrian conflict could free up both nations to support the Ottomans. The Grand Vizier moved twenty thousand men to Tartitz to threaten the Russians, and Bagration attacked these positions on 22 October. The Russians were initially able to capture the Ottoman trenches, but counterattacks, aided by Albanian reinforcements commanded by Ali Pasha's son, pushed the Russians back. The failure to destroy the relief army meant the siege had to be abandoned, and Bagration withdrew to Girsov. The final stages of the 1809 campaign saw the Russians capture Braila, Bagration's last success of the war. Alexander was furious at Bagration for retreating towards the Danube. With winter weather arriving, communications and supplies were difficult to maintain, and Bagration begged the Tsar to allow him to withdraw into Wallachia. The Tsar reluctantly agreed, and Bagration resigned on health grounds, being replaced by Count Kamensky.

1st Serbian Revolt

In 1801 the janissaries in Belgrade, led by the four *dahi* (*dahije*)[15], murdered the popular reforming governor Haci Mustafa, known as the 'mother of the Serbs'. Being geographically far from the modest reforms initiated in Istanbul by Sultan Selim III allowed conservative elements to resist what they perceived as threats to Ottoman tradition. The janissaries relied on the growing tax farming system (*citluk*), which damaged the sipahi who sought to retain the traditional timar estates. The Serbian peasants enjoyed hereditary rights and some legal protection on these estates, a relatively enlightened arrangement coupled with some limited engagement through the election of representatives (*knez*) to the local council (*knezevina*). However, a draconian taxation on pigs, an important export, undermined peasant income. By 1804, the peasants and sipahi had formed armed units to protect themselves against the janissaries, many abandoning the land to live off banditry in the forests. Some of these *hajduci* had served with the Habsburg army in the last war with the Ottomans and, through their contacts, arranged for weapons to be smuggled across the border.

The dahi learned of plans to instigate a rebellion and decided to strike first. One Serbian priest, Hadzi-Ruvim, was tortured by having his flesh peeled off with plyers, and when he refused to talk was beheaded. This started the 'slaughter of the *knezes*', in which between 70 and 120 *knezes* and hundreds more peasants were killed, precipitating the Serbian revolt, which united Muslim sipahi and Christian peasants against the janissaries. The military leader was one of the *hajduci*, Djordje Petrović, known as Karadjordje (Black George). He distinguished himself during the Austro-Turkish War (1788–1791) as a member of the Serbian Free Corps. After the war, he fled to Austria, then returned to Serbia in 1794 and became a livestock manager. His forces, combined with an army sent by the Sultan from Bosnia, captured and executed the *dahis* in August 1804, although janissary units resisted for another year.

The revolt had created some 20,000-30,000 armed Serbs, a powerful Christian force within the empire. They were organised into small bands that attacked Ottoman properties in a vicious war of retribution. They were joined by Serb refugees from Bosnia and Vidin, the victims of reprisals who formed units known as the *beskućnici* (the homeless). As the Ottomans retreated into fortifications, it became apparent that the irregular nature of these bands was unsuited for the discipline of siege warfare. 'Someone else would capture a cow or a mare from the Turks, and take that home; another would buy some booty and go away and sell it; yet another would get bored and just sitting with nothing to do, and go home to reap the corn or look after the rest of the harvesting.'[16] The regional *knezes* also resisted attempts to centralise power in a monarchy as proposed by Karadjordje. Fierce infighting was typical, undermining the necessary unity of purpose.

The Sultan demanded an end to this disorder once the janissaries had been dealt with. In the summer of 1805, he sent an army to Serbia to put down the revolt, but it was defeated at Nis on 18 August 1805. The Porte declared 'Holy War' the following year and sent an army of forty thousand men with French advisors. At the Battle of Mišar on 12 August 1806, around seven thousand Serbian infantry and two thousand cavalry held off repeated Ottoman attacks over four days. A counterattack by Serbian cavalry then broke the Ottoman centre, causing a general collapse.

Battle of Misar (Afanasij Scheloumoff, public domain)

Karadjordje demanded a high level of autonomy for Serbia. The Sultan was prepared to make concessions, but when the Russians occupied Wallachia in

1806, they contacted the Serbian leader, offering money and weapons. Before the Russians could intervene, the Ottomans sent a new army into Serbia under Ibrahim Pasha, including troops from the newly formed *nizam-i cedit* regiments. The Serbian army faced them at Deligrad on 6 December 1806, behind entrenchments and palisades. The Ottomans attacked over four days, suffering heavy casualties. Having failed to break through to Belgrade, Ibrahim was forced to negotiate a six-week truce. This allowed the Serbs to complete the liberation of the country.

The Serbs celebrated the Russian arrival with an oath: 'To fight for the faith together with Russians, the Genuine Cross and the Orthodox Russian Grail.'[17] A revolt in the Balkans now took on an international aspect, with the French urging the Ottomans to resist the Serbs and the Russians. By relying on the Russians, Serbia became dependent on the wider conflict and, in 1807, gratefully received the support of fifteen hundred Russian troops under Major General Isaev. Joining with the Serbian commander Milenko-Stojkovich and his five thousand men, they defeated Molla Pasha at the Stubik River, forcing them to retreat to Vidin. The Ottomans responded in 1809 with a major offensive, defeating the Serbs at Cegar Hill and then at Deligrad in August. The Ottoman commander decapitated several hundred Serbs and erected a 'Tower of Skulls'; one scholar claimed its remains still existed in the 1970s.

Meanwhile, Isaev crossed the Danube with six battalions and two Cossack regiments to join one thousand Serbs for an assault on Kladovo on 21 July 1809. Six different columns attacked the fortress from both land and the river. The Malorossiisk Grenadiers almost breached the walls, but their reinforcements got lost, and the assault failed. As Isaev withdrew back across the Danube, the Serbs felt betrayed by Russia as they had refused two peace offers from the Porte. The Russians withdrew further towards Austria, exposing their Wallachian right flank.

The Serbs were left isolated when Russia abandoned the Balkans in 1812 to deal with the French invasion. Then, in the autumn of 1813, three large Ottoman armies descended on Belgrade, and Karadjordje fled to Austria with around one hundred thousand people.

Adriatic manoeuvres

The British, meanwhile, were flailing around the Mediterranean in search of a strategy. After the failure at Istanbul, they landed a force in Egypt. This had the effect of uniting the Ottoman governor and the Mamelukes against the British force, which was bottled up in Alexandria before retreating ignominiously to Sicily on 25 September 1807. The arrival of Sir John Moore in Sicily with reinforcements strengthened the island's defences enough to deter a planned French invasion. He left the competent Major General John Sherbrooke in command, who neutralised the machinations of the court to secure the island.

Napoleon kept his enemies guessing with a much-publicised trip to Venice in November 1807. He announced a range of public works, including new shore defences and plans to dredge the lagoon so ships of the line could sail out. His trip was not all work though. The beautiful Countess Nahir de Luisignan, described as 'a harmony of curves', was asked to follow him there away from the disapproving eyes of his sister Elisa. The Venetian noble families were stroked while he made plans to tax them for the improvements and for his campaign in Spain. The presence of Berthier and Murat made it seem that Napoleon was planning a thrust south. Lord Collingwood noted from Corfu, 'From the great preparations fleets and armies are making in the Adriatic and Bonaparte's arrival in Venice, I have little doubt of their destination being this place'[18].

In early 1808, Napoleon decided that reinforcing Corfu and the Adriatic was more important than Sicily, particularly as Joseph had been unable to capture the remaining footholds on the mainland. So he ordered Admiral Ganteaume to gather a fleet from several ports and enter the Mediterranean. Unfortunately, bad weather meant the fleet never fully combined. Still, Ganteaume managed to arrive at Corfu with six ships of the line, strengthening the garrison under General Donzelot to around eight thousand men. Donzelot had joined the French army as a private before the revolution, rising quickly through the ranks after distinguishing himself in campaigns on the Rhine, Egypt and Italy, where he was promoted to general of division. As military governors go, he was reasonably popular with the local population and commanded Corfu until 1814. When his library was captured by a British frigate, the captain returned it; Ganteaume would later treat captured British officers as his guests. He went on to command a division at Waterloo.

According to British reports, the garrison was nearer six thousand troops, of which some thirty-five hundred to four thousand were French[19]. The difference in numbers is probably due to the British discounting Albanians. Ganteaume sailed back to Toulon, leaving *Uranie* (40) at Corfu, avoiding some ineffective attempts by Collingwood's fleet to intercept them. Thus, a French fleet had freely sailed across the Mediterranean for two months without being caught.

In May 1808, the Royal Navy sloop *Saracen* liaised with Count Cladan of Cephalonia, who indicated that the inhabitants were ready to revolt. Collingwood was less convinced of the Count's influence and pointed to the need for a permanent garrison able to defend against the large French force in Corfu.

There was better news for the Royal Navy in the summer of 1808. Napoleon's replacement of King Ferdinand of Spain by his brother Joseph brought Spain into the war on the British side. In August, Wellington defeated the French in Portugal, starting the Peninsular War. This took the Spanish navy out of the reckoning in the Mediterranean, although it also meant that resources would be focused on Spain. British frigates kept a watch on Venice, while another squadron led by *Standard* (64) blockaded Corfu.

This period included one of the hardest-fought frigate actions of the Napoleonic Wars. On 6 July 1808, HMS *Seahorse* (38), an *Artois*-class frigate commanded by Captain Stewart, fought the Ottoman frigate *Bedr-i Zafer* (*Badere Zaffere*) (50), commanded by Kapundane Küçük Ali, off the island of Chiliodromia (Alonissos) in the northern Aegean. The Ottoman vessel *Alis Fezzan* (26) was also present. *Bedr-i Zafer* unusually had two 36-pounders on the gun deck, flanked by two 24-pounders, with the remainder being 18-pounders or smaller. *Seahorse* had twenty-eight 18-pounders, four 9-pounders and two 32-pounder carronades. *Seahorse* manoeuvred to fire broadsides into the Ottoman ships, avoiding a boarding action in which they would have been outnumbered two to one. The gunpowder below *Alis Fezzan*'s forecastle exploded, causing the ship to catch fire, and she abandoned the action. *Bedr-i Zafer* suffered two more hours of bombardment, which reduced the ship to a complete wreck.

The British discontinued the action overnight, and at first light, the Ottoman captain still refused to surrender. However, after a raking broadside, the crew seized the captain and the colours were lowered. *Bedr-i Zafer* lost 165 men killed and a further 195 wounded. *Seahorse* lost her mizzenmast along with five dead and ten wounded[20]. The King authorised the issue of a gold medal to Captain Stewart for the action; only eighteen battles or actions qualified for such an award. In 1847 the Admiralty authorised the issue of the Naval General Service Medal with clasp 'Seahorse with Badere Zaffere' to all the surviving claimants from the action. This action inspired the fictional encounter in Patrick O'Brian's Jack Aubrey book, *Ionian Mission*.

HMS *Seahorse* capturing *Bedr-i Zafer* (Thomas Buttersworth, public domain)

Austria rejoined the conflict in the War of the Fifth Coalition in April 1809. There were plans to recover Venice and turn Italy into what Spain later became: a drain on French military power by using British sea power. However, these hopes were checked in central Europe at the Battle of Aspern-Essling (21-22 May) and ended at Wagram on 5-6 July. The Treaty of Schonbrunn (12 October) brought the Austrians closer to France by marrying the Emperor's daughter Marie Louise to Napoleon. However, the treaty also resulted in further loss of Austrian territory in the Adriatic, including Trieste, Carniola, Istria and most of the Croatian lands.

Napoleon reorganised these territories into the Illyrian Provinces, technically part of France although the inhabitants held Illyrian, not French, citizenship. Napoleon appointed Auguste de Marmont, Duke of Ragusa, as the first governor, although he was already the military governor of Dalmatia.

We first met Marmont leading French troops into Dalmatia and Austria. He was the son of an army officer and met Napoleon when he entered the artillery corps. He became Napoleon's aide-de-camp in Italy and Egypt, and returned with him commanding the artillery at Marengo. He held that post until 1810, when he succeeded Massena in command of the French army in Northern Spain. He lost the Battle of Salamanca, where he was wounded, and then recovered to command a corps in the 1813 and 1814 campaigns before abandoning Napoleon and supporting the restoration. While he failed in the Peninsular War, his overall military record was impressive. In particular, in the Dalmatian campaign he made what John Elting calls 'a remarkable 300-mile march through frequently roadless country, scattering two Austrian forces.'[21]

Auguste de Marmont, Duke of Ragusa (Jacques-Luc Barbier-Walbonne, public domain)

Marmont's Illyrian governorship was an appointment not without its challenges, given the geography of the area, and the different religions and nationalities of the inhabitants. Marmont wanted Trieste to be the province's capital, but Napoleon favoured Ljubljana (the capital of modern-day Slovenia) due to its proximity to the Austrian border. Marmont's staff included interpreters for seven different languages. Napoleon appointed Joseph Coffinhal-Dunoyer to impose the French legal system on the Illyrian provinces in 1811; this was a clear sign of a hardening of direct French rule, as he abandoned the gradualist approach of the previous governor. However, the geography of the province was a serious impediment to reforms, which were limited mainly to the Dalmatian coast, and even there suffered from a clash of cultures and a lack of qualified officials. The economy suffered severely, particularly in Carniola, due to the loss of traditional trade within Austria. The province also had to finance the cost of French administration and fund war reparations. Even the promised (but not delivered) abolition of serfdom failed to stop several peasant uprisings. Cultural reforms, including the teaching of the Slovene language in primary schools, were welcomed, but these were mainly of interest to intellectuals. There was more support for the French in Dalmatia. Still, even there, liberal reforms did not balance out the economic impact of war and taxation.

CHAPTER FIVE

FRANCE ON THE DEFENSIVE 1810-15

Russo-Turkish War 1809-12

The Russo-Turkish War kicked off again in the spring of 1809. The Grand Vizier Kör Yusef crossed the Danube with an army of forty thousand, but was pushed back by Langeron. Kör Yusef was first appointed Grand Vizier in October 1798, so this was his second term in the post, serving two sultans. He was a Georgian from birth and climbed the Ottoman career ladder from clerk to governor. He led the Ottoman forces that, with the British, removed the French from Egypt, and became commander in chief of Ottoman forces in the east. He was dismissed during the Russo-Turkish War but was later appointed to further military posts before he died in Chios in 1819.

In the winter, Kamensky and Langeron crossed the Danube and captured Silistre and Bazarcik before being pushed back into Wallachia with significant losses. In the spring of 1811, Kutuzov was appointed commander of the Russian army on the Danube, albeit reduced to 42,240 men in four divisions, as troops were withdrawn in anticipation of a French attack. It was the Ottomans who took the initiative, with Ismail Bey and twenty-five thousand men crossing into Wallachia towards Craiova while the new Grand Vizier Ahmed threatened Ruscuk. In a daylong battle outside the fortress, Kutuzov prevailed with a decisive combined infantry and cavalry assault. Despite the victory, he withdrew his forces to more defensible positions across the Danube. Ahmed tried again on 8 September 1811 with a crossing at Slobozia, where he entrenched part of his army. Kutuzov crossed the river and defeated the Ottomans, leaving some thirty-six thousand of them stranded on the left bank of the Danube. They effectively became Russian prisoners as peace negotiations started.

The Ottoman Empire was in a weak position to return to war, and the Russians wanted a deal so they could focus on Napoleon. A French proposal to launch a joint attack from Poland was rejected as the Ottomans had not forgotten what they regarded as French treachery at Tilsit. Alexander seriously considered a plan from Admiral Chichagov, who had replaced Kutuzov in May, for a multiethnic army of 150,000, including Serbians, to attack Austrian and French Dalmatia[1]. This exceedingly ambitious plan fell apart once Chichagov grasped the practicalities of warfare in the Balkans. The Treaty of Bucharest was signed on 28 May 1812; the Russians, watching Napoleon's forces gather in central Europe, wanted to avoid a war on two fronts. The French ambassador had informed the Porte that war between France and Russia was imminent, and Napoleon was proposing an alliance with the Ottomans, although his instructions were ambiguous[2]. The modest Russian gains of the province of Bessarabia constituted a reasonable outcome, as it included five key fortresses that had held up previous Russian invasions, and the port of Odessa. Tsar Alexander proclaimed the treaty 'the God's given peace'. The Ottomans were grateful to have escaped from a disastrous war relatively lightly. They were also determined on a policy of neutrality to avoid any involvement in a broader European conflict. This meant Napoleon's offer of an alliance held no attraction, quite apart from their mistrusting him based on past experience.

British Adriatic Offensive

The Royal Navy was Britain's primary tool for what today we would call power projection, and it usually took precedence in resource allocation. It was easily the most successful force of its era, with only one ship of the line lost and not retaken, compared to the French navy's loss of 90 ships. At its maximum strength in 1810, it deployed 152 ships of the line and 183 cruisers, which was more than those of all the other major naval powers combined. It was distributed in fleets worldwide, defending Britain's growing empire and threatening its enemies' trading routes. However, the navy had its challenges, not least a shortage of good timber to build ships and sailors to operate them. A Royal Navy ship of this period had a diverse crew of many nationalities, not all of whom were there voluntarily! As Brian Lavery puts it, 'The Royal Navy of 1793 to 1815 reflected the society which created it. Life in the navy was hard, punishments were cruel, and death was never far away. The navy also reflected the morals and values of British culture—the class system, the political ethos, and the ambiguous attitudes to liberty.'[3]

The Adriatic came under the purview of the British Mediterranean Fleet, which in 1808 had around eighty ships, including twenty-five ships of the line. There had been a small Royal Navy squadron in the Adriatic since 1806, commanded by Captain Campbell in the frigate *Unité*. His task was to observe French activity in Venice, liaise with the Austrians in Trieste, and interdict French naval traffic. His arrival was welcomed by Britain's local agents, who had despaired of the Russian fleet's inability to prevent French troops moving from Italy to Dalmatia[4]. He succeeded in closing the ports of Trieste, Fiume and Ragusa and seized timber destined for the Venice shipyards. However, Campbell was prone to cutting corners with prizes by selling them locally rather than detaching crews to sail them to Malta—a practice that eventually got him recalled[5].

With the departure of the Russian fleet in 1807, the Royal Navy stepped up its operations in the Adriatic. Vice-Admiral Collingwood, commanding the Mediterranean fleet, was determined to show Napoleon that the Adriatic was not a French lake. The main French bases were at Venice and Ancona, and the easiest way to supply the garrisons in Dalmatia and the Ionian Islands was by sea. The land routes were slow and went down the coast, making them susceptible to intervention on land and sea by the Royal Navy. Napoleon gave Marmont a credit of four hundred thousand francs to improve the roads. He invited his men to 'take the pickaxe, the spade and the trowel', invoking the example of Roman armies[6]. Three hundred kilometres of roads were built this way between 1807 and 1808, with sections numbered after the regiments that produced them.

Control of the Adriatic allowed Britain to communicate with and supply allies, disrupt enemy trade, procure their supplies (particularly Croatian timber) and encourage revolts against French rule. The Admiralty also wanted to restrict French shipbuilding capacity, which threatened British naval supremacy. The main concern was Venice, whose dilapidated fleet provided a few seaworthy ships, and its famous Arsenal shipyard. The problem with monitoring Venice was the shallow waters at the entrance to the lagoon, which meant large ships of the line had to be floated out without guns. Despite this challenge, the Royal Navy had to watch Venice regularly.

The Adriatic was the ideal theatre of operations for ambitious naval officers prepared to use their initiative, far from the direction of senior commanders. Instructions from the Admiralty in London could take between six and eight weeks to arrive. Royal Navy small ship captains captured ships at sea and landed on the coast to attack supply convoys, signal towers and gun batteries. As highlighted earlier, the reports of the prize court in Malta show how profitable this could be for captains and crews. The system was intended to raise morale and defray the cost of the navy. Still, as everyone took a share, it could also have a corrupting effect and devastate the local economy[7]. There was an excellent relationship with local army commanders, who would often propose joint operations or lend some infantry for a scheme a naval captain would dream up. As Glover puts it, 'A "can do" approach also bred innate confidence, which further engendered the belief that they could not fail. With such confidence, they rarely failed, even when the odds looked hopelessly stacked against them. Such victories simply drove them on, whilst any setbacks were simply put down to bad luck.'[8]

In August 1807, HMS *Weasel*, an 18-gun sloop-brig under Captain Clavell, was patrolling near Corfu when the French garrison arrived to take over from the Russians. In 24 hours, she destroyed seven enemy vessels, capturing 250 soldiers and the French despatches. After that, the Adriatic became a popular 'hunting ground' for British frigate captains. HMS *Porcupine* (24) captured or destroyed over forty enemy vessels in two months off the Bay of Cattaro and raided Ragusa harbour, destroying artillery and military stores. The most famous frigate captain to serve in the Adriatic was Captain William Hoste of HMS *Amphion* (32), which arrived in the Mediterranean in February 1808 and returned in early 1809 with HMS *Redwing* (18). Earlier, Collingwood said that Hoste 'must take a French frigate before the winter is over.' To this, Hoste added pointedly in a letter to his father that 'I am still in hopes I shall make some cash.'[9] In the first quarter of 1808, Hoste alone took thirty-eight merchant ships and burnt another six. However, he was disappointed with the £6,000 (worth £516,000 today) prize money. His gains were not just cash—he also captured a beautiful young Parisienne on her way to Italy, where her husband served in the French Army.

Captain William Hoste (*Service Afloat*, author's collection)

The frigate was the Royal Navy's glamour ship, big enough to carry significant firepower but fast enough to evade larger enemies. The light cavalry of the seas, patrolling, scouting and above all, fighting. As Nelson put it, they were 'the eyes of the fleet'. They often fought ship-to-ship actions, which made frigate captains famous through contemporary press coverage and even today through the fictional stories of Hornblower and others. As in the Adriatic, they often operated alone, while the larger ships of the line typically operated in squadrons or fleets to blockade enemy ports. A good illustration of this comes from the Jack Aubrey novels by Patrick O'Brian. In *Ionian Mission*, Aubrey is in command of a 74-gun ship on blockade duty. The story moves painfully slowly, only picking up when he transfers to a frigate for his mission into the Adriatic.

A frigate was built with an unarmed lower deck, which meant it could heel considerably and carry sail even in strong winds. It could maintain higher speeds in lighter winds and keep its gun ports open longer. At the outset of the Napoleonic Wars, the 32-gun frigate armed with 12-pounder guns was common. However, frigates became larger with heavier 18- and then 24-pounder guns, and carronades. They also began carrying more guns, with thirty-two, thirty-six, thirty-eight, and finally, forty guns. Many frigates in service with the Royal Navy were captured from the enemy, including 143 from the French during the revolutionary wars alone. In 1801, a third of Royal Navy frigates were foreign-built. When frigates patrolled, things happened. Hoste once reported to Admiral Fremantle, 'For those last forty-eight hours we have been doing nothing but burning, sinking and destroying the enemy's vessels.'[10]

Not all prizes were taken at sea. Royal Navy ships would launch boats and sail them into harbours to cut out enemy vessels. Boats were traditionally hoisted using tackles, but this was cumbersome and slow. By the late 1790s, davits were fitted on larger ships for hoisting lighter boats, allowing them to be lifted more easily and quickly. By 1805 the fitting of davits was commonplace, and boats hoisted by them came to be called quarter-boats[11]. Frigates had several quarter-boats as well as a larger launch. Carronades were mounted in them, and seamen trained in the use of small arms manned them, while marines provided the disciplined firepower.

In June 1808, the Royal Navy frigates in the Adriatic were joined by HMS *Standard* (64). Sailing off Corfu, they prevented supplies from entering the fortress. Coastal shipping almost ceased operating, and whole battalions had to be allocated to protect French ships and harbours. Supplies had to go through the mountain tracks of the interior, notorious for banditry. This British control of the sea was exploited by Maltese smugglers, often using Lissa (Vis), who brought sugar from Bosnia and silk from Italy, breaching Napoleon's continental blockade. The Royal Navy was joined by Maltese, Sicilian and Dalmatian privateers that focussed on smaller ships, forcing the French to organise convoys protected by gunboats.

A typical action was the storming of Cortellazzo at the mouth of the river Piave, where the French had stationed a flotilla of gunboats. Having remained out of sight of land all day, Hoste attacked in the early morning with *Amphion*'s armed boats, blowing up the fort, spiking the guns, and cutting out the gunboats and trabaccoli. Not a single member of his crew was killed. By the end of the year, Hoste was once again on his own when the ships of the line withdrew from the Adriatic. His ship had taken or destroyed 218 enemy vessels, although he complained that it 'has not put much cash in our pockets, owing to the difficulty attending their being sent to port.' The prize port was Malta, and the difficulty in getting prizes there was due to both the shortage of British seamen to make up prize crews and the poor weather. His frigate and one sloop were able to operate despite the French having three frigates, two brigs, and two schooners at Ancona, and one frigate, three brigs, and two schooners at Venice.

In January 1809, Britain and the Ottoman Empire signed a peace deal. This brought the good relations Captain Leake had built with Ali Pasha to fruition, causing the French further headaches inland. The treaty still left the Royal Navy without a port to supply and refit their ships, as Malta was seven hundred miles away. The army eventually agreed to provide eighteen hundred troops commanded by Colonel Oswald. With a squadron of three ships, *Magnificent* (74), *Belle-Poule* (38) and *Imogene* (16), they attacked the southernmost of the Ionian Islands, starting at Zante. Colonel Hudson Lowe led six hundred men from the 35th Foot, Corsican Rangers, and Greek Light Infantry ashore. They quickly arrived in the town, where seven hundred Italian and Albanian troops in French service surrendered. Major John Slessor of the 35th Foot was appointed commandant of the island with a garrison of the 1st Battalion, 35th Foot and foreign auxiliary corps. Cephalonia was captured next with two hundred prisoners, followed by Cerigo (Kythira) and Ithica.

Having established themselves in the Ionian Islands in 1809, the British planned a larger operation against Santa Maura (Lefkada, Lefkas) in early 1810. The island and fortress are linked to the mainland by several small strips of land that create a natural lagoon. Colonel Oswald, commanding twenty-five hundred men from the 35th Foot, 44th Foot (two hundred officers and men)[12], Calabrian Free Corps, Corsican Rangers, De Roll's Regiment, and Greek Light Infantry and marines, landed near the main town of Amaxichi (Lefkada), capturing the shore batteries. The French garrison commanded by General Camus was sixteen hundred strong, but around six hundred locally-raised troops deserted when he concentrated his forces in the fortress. Captain (then Major) Church and the Greek Light Infantry captured one of the redoubts holding the spit of land that was the only access to the fortress. He described the fortress as 'that diabolical castle seated like a magician's fortress in the middle of the sea.'[13]

Richard Church in the uniform of the Greek Light
Infantry (Denis Dighton, public domain)

The other redoubt was a tougher proposition, and the Greek attack lost momentum. Major Clarke was commanded to take a composite battalion of six hundred men, who broke through the defences, forcing the French to flee. Colonel Hudson Lowe[14] took advantage of the confusion to lead the 35th Foot and the Corsicans across a narrow causeway, capturing the redoubt. The French now withdrew to the fortress, and a formal siege began. Oswald requested additional troops and heavy artillery from Sicily. When they arrived, Oswald started to batter the walls, and a surprise attack on an outwork caused further French casualties. With the garrison demoralised by losses and sickness, General Camus then agreed to surrender. He later died in Russia during the 1812 retreat, far from the balmy climes of the Adriatic. The British suffered 165 casualties, including Major Clarke, who General Oswald commended as 'an officer whose early exploits and distinguished qualities promised to render him one of its brightest ornaments.'[15]

While other islands could have been taken, Collingwood did not want to waste troops garrisoning islands with no naval value. Zante had a safe harbour and, from there, could intercept ships entering the Adriatic. It became the British headquarters with a garrison commanded by Colonel Wilder. This left the French governor, General Donzelot, holding Corfu with a four-thousand-strong garrison and a population of forty-five thousand. The British assessment of Corfu was that 'French engineering during the last three years has rendered the fortress of Corfu impregnable to every power in Europe but Great Britain owing to her naval superiority.'[16] It would take a force of four or five thousand to capture it, which was not available. Britain's shortage of troops would bedevil its operations in the Mediterranean for most of the war.

On 3 March 1810, Admiral Lord Collingwood died while returning to England after resigning his post due to ill health. Nelson's great friend was buried next to him in St Paul's Cathedral. He was replaced in July by Admiral Sir Charles Cotton. However, in June 1811, Cotton returned to command the Channel Fleet, and he was replaced by Vice Admiral Sir Edward Pellew, himself a famous frigate squadron commander.

Command of the Adriatic frigate squadron had already been vested in Captain William Hoste in HMS *Amphion* (32) plus *Active* (38), *Cerebus* (32) and the sloop *Acorn* (18). Hoste came from Norfolk and had served under Nelson on HMS *Theseus*, although he had missed Trafalgar on a diplomatic mission to Algiers. He had already made a reputation as a bold and successful frigate commander. Within a month, his new squadron had taken or destroyed forty-six vessels. HMS *Amphion* was a small frigate compared to the newer frigates built by the French and the Americans. But she was made of English oak to high specifications and had taken two years to build. Hoste considered *Amphion* 'one of the finest and most desirable ships', especially as it was the choice and gift of Nelson[17]. He also had an experienced crew, including Donat Henchy O'Brien, who was amazingly reunited with *Amphion* when he was picked up in a boat off Trieste after escaping from prison at Bitche (northeastern France) and journeying across Europe. His memoirs tell a story that would grace the pages of a Hornblower novel[18].

Useful though Zante was as a naval base, it was still some way from the main operational areas along the Dalmatian coast. The Royal Navy, along with Maltese and Sicilian privateers, needed somewhere closer where they could rest crews, refit ships and collect supplies from the coastal communities. The French were also having problems maintaining their rule over the independent-minded population, and a nearby base would be useful to help stir up revolts. The Adriatic coast has hundreds of islands, but few have good ports. The Royal Navy settled on Lissa (Vis), which has an excellent natural harbour at Port Santa Giorgio (Vis town today) and a smaller one at Comisa (Komiža). The island was too far from the coast for the French to garrison properly[19]. It had a population of 4,000-5,000 people sympathetic to the British. Campbell had recommended the island as a base in May 1808. Hoste had been using Lissa as a secure anchorage since early 1809, but it had no garrison or fortifications. Royal Navy ships regularly used the harbour, as did Sicilian and Maltese privateers flying the British flag. It was also a convenient base for merchant ships smuggling goods into Austrian, Ottoman and French territories. Hoste had even established a cricket club on some rare flat ground near a sixteenth-century monastery; a tradition followed during the British occupation in the Second World War, and even today there is still a cricket pitch in the centre of the island[20]. There is also a cemetery at the eastern end of the harbour bay which contains British graves from the Napoleonic era.

The harbour at Lissa (Vis Town) (Author)

Napoleon took a personal interest in the Adriatic due to its impact on French coastal trade and supply routes. He ordered his Viceroy in Italy, Eugene Beauharnais, to attack Lissa. He tapped Captain Bernard Dubourdieu who commanded French naval forces in the Adriatic for the task. The son of a master cooper, he went to sea at sixteen, and then joined the navy in 1792. He saw active service in the Mediterranean on the frigate *La Topaze*, but his ship was captured by Hood at Toulon and Dubourdieu was sent to Gibraltar as a prisoner. After eighteen months, he engineered a daring escape by swimming to a small sailing boat in the harbour. He then collected twenty other prisoners from the prison hulk before capturing the seagoing transport ship *Le Temple* (10), sailing it to Lorient. He was captured again two years later and released in 1799. He ran the British blockade of Egypt and fought in the West Indies before being promoted to *capitaine de frégate* in 1806. The following year in the Mediterranean, his frigate took thirteen British prizes, earning him a promotion to *capitaine de vaisseau* (equivalent of post-captain). In 1809, he won the Cross of the *Légion d'honneur* for bravery in a frigate duel, which brought him to Napoleon's attention.

For the assault on Lissa, Dubourdieu assembled a squadron of three frigates, two corvettes and two brigs. He sailed from Ancona on 17 October 1810, having heard from a fisherman that the British squadron had left Lissa to sail southwards. Hoste thought the French were heading for Corfu. Dubourdieu arrived at Lissa on 21 October without encountering any Royal Navy ships, landed seven hundred troops, and took the port. He claimed to have taken around thirty prizes and destroyed another sixty-four vessels. Hoste later reported that three prizes had been taken and five privateers sunk. After spotting unknown sails approaching the island, Dubourdieu burned three privateers and scuttled back to Ancona with his merchant prizes. Napoleon was not impressed, but French propaganda claimed a major victory. Whilst this was exaggerated, Hoste was embarrassed as his report would take time to get home. He headed to Ancona but found the French squadron safely under the port's guns. To add to his embarrassment, *Amphion* collided with the smaller *Volage* (22), which had recently replaced *Cerebus*, badly damaging both ships. Hoste had to take both ships to Malta for repairs that took two months.

In February 1811, Napoleon ordered another attack on Lissa, with clear instructions to garrison the island. Dubourdieu left Ancona on 11 March with six frigates, *Favorite*, *Flore*, *Danae* and *Corona* (all 44-gun), *Bellona* and *Carolina* (both 32-gun), and five smaller ships carrying four hundred troops. This time Hoste was waiting for him with four ships, *Active* (38), *Amphion* (32), *Cerberus* (32) and *Volage* (22). Despite being outnumbered, Hoste sailed his squadron in a tight line of sail, leaving no room for the French to break through. He hoisted the message 'Remember Nelson', and the sailors in the following ships sprang into the rigging and cheered. Hornby of *Volage* exulted, 'Never again so long as I live shall I see so interesting or so glorious a moment.'

Dubourdieu also wanted a Nelsonian pell-mell battle where he could deploy his superior manpower rather than rely on the firepower from his inexperienced crews. However, the first broadside killed Dubourdieu on board his frigate *Favorite*, which then ran aground. The crew and soldiers marched towards the lightly defended town but were persuaded to surrender to the defence force.

At sea, superior British seamanship and gunnery resulted in two French frigates being captured and another burned, while *Flore*, *Danae* and *Carolina* escaped with most of the smaller ships. British losses totalled 50 killed and 132 wounded, with *Amphion*'s crew suffering the most. This was an outstanding victory, which gave the British almost uncontested control of the Adriatic. Hoste returned to England via Malta with his prizes in July, with none other than Lord Byron as a passenger in *Volage*, to much praise but little in the way of honours or gold. Byron's 'Farewell to Malta' included the lines:

> While either Adriatic shore,
> And fallen chiefs and fleets no more,
> And nightly smiles and daily dinners,
> Proclaim you war and woman's winners.

Battle of Lissa (Robert Dodd, public domain)

After the Battle of Lissa, command in the Adriatic fell to Captain James Brisbane, who continued to attack French convoys. One such attack is known as the 'Action of 29 November 1811'. The commander of the Lissa squadron was Captain Murray Maxwell on the frigate HMS *Alceste* (38) with HMS *Active* (38), HMS *Unite* (36), HMS *Acorn* (20) and HMS *Kingfisher* (18). He received a signal that a French convoy was heading north from Corfu, carrying a cargo of some two hundred cannon to Trieste. Maxwell set sail, leaving *Acorn* and marines at Lissa. The French convoy was commanded by Commodore François-Gilles Montfort on *Pauline* (40), with *Pomone* (40) and *Persanne* (26). The French convoy was sighted near the island of Lastovo, and Montfort ordered his ships to make full sail to avoid pursuit. However, *Persanne* could not keep pace with the faster frigates and broke off, being pursued by *Unite*. The French ship, which was primarily a store ship, was heavily outgunned and surrendered after a token broadside. The main action developed into separate duels between *Active* and *Pomone,* and *Alceste* and *Pauline*. *Pomone* suffered heavy damage, as did *Active*, with her captain (James Gordon) having his leg blown off. When HMS *Kingfisher* appeared on the horizon, Montfort decided that he could no longer protect the battered *Pomone* and sailed away in *Pauline*, which the British ships were too damaged to pursue. Instead, they concentrated their fire on *Pomone*, which, after losing her masts, surrendered. This ending is captured in the painting by Pierre Julien Gilbert on the cover of this book. James Henderson argues that this action convinced Napoleon of his inability to control the Adriatic Sea, which was vital to launching operations in the Balkans. This may have been 'the last factor' in his decision to abandon plans to invade the Ottoman Empire and instead turn his attention to Russia[21]. However, this is somewhat speculative, as it was Tsar Alexander who issued an ultimatum to Napoleon that led to the 1812 invasion.

Even after these actions, there was still a reluctance to garrison Lissa due to a chronic shortage of manpower. Captain Griffiths with HMS *Leonidas* had mounted a small battery on the entrance to the harbour in May 1811, and this work was continued by Captain Maxwell of HMS *Alceste*. Captain Bennet of the Royal Engineers surveyed the island and recommended a garrison of around four hundred men and a few gunboats, although they would need fortifications if the navy were drawn away. After much debate,[22] it was not until the end of April 1812 that British forces reached Lissa. Lt. Colonel Robertson of the Sicilian regiment was appointed to command a force of two hundred men from the 35th Foot, two hundred Corsican Rangers, one hundred Swiss from Roll's Regiment, and one hundred from the Calabrian Free Corps, together with thirty artillerymen and engineers. Even by Mediterranean army standards, this was a cobbled-together force. However, with French troops being withdrawn for the invasion of Russia, the real risk of attack had passed. The garrison did free up the navy to take a more aggressive policy, and a small shipyard allowed refits to be completed without going to Malta. The garrison also began work on fortifications, including Fort George and three large towers: Bentinck, Wellington, and Robertson, which can be seen to this day, with some Austrian additions. The small island in the harbour, which had a round tower, was renamed Hoste Island. As Hardy puts it, 'The story of British fortifications on Lissa ends with the all too familiar theme of a project begun too late with many misgivings, which ran over schedule and over budget, before being given up before it was finished as being unnecessary and too expensive.'[23]

Fort George (Author)

Around this time a new French ship was built in Venice, named *Rivoli* (74). It could have contested the waters around Lissa, but it was damaged while passing through the shallows of the Venetian lagoon. British intelligence reports also mentioned two other ships of the line, *Mont-St Bernardo* and *Regentoire*. In early 1812 *Rivoli* (Commodore Barre) was repaired and was lifted over the shallows on air bags called camels before being fitted out for war. A 74-gun ship of the line would radically change the balance of power in the Adriatic, so the British responded by sending HMS *Victorious* (74) and

HMS *Weazel* (18) to blockade Venice. *Rivoli* and three brigs, *Jena* (18), *Mercure* (18), and *Mamelouck* (10), escaped the blockade in fog, but were chased down by *Weazel*, whose gunfire blew up *Mercure*. The two ships of the line then fought a running battle for three hours before *Rivoli* was forced to surrender. The badly damaged ship was towed to Lissa, where it was repaired and joined the Royal Navy.

This victory meant open season on French and Italian shipping in the Adriatic, with considerable prize money going to Royal Navy captains and crew. The Royal Navy also engaged French positions on both sides of the Adriatic, interdicting roads and destroying gun batteries and port facilities. The Royal Navy's new commander in the Adriatic, Admiral Freemantle, did not ignore the risk of further French ships of the line emerging from the Venice shipyards. He dispatched his three ships of the line, *Milford* (74), *Eagle* (74) and *Achille* (74), northwards, two to watch Venice and one to be based at Lissa. While ships of the line were not suited for commerce raiding, they did launch boats to cut out French convoys, and even boarded larger gunboats acting as escorts. HMS *Eagle* under Captain Charles Rowley was one of the more successful captains engaged in attacking convoys.

French garrisons were being depleted to feed French armies in central Europe, leaving mostly local militias. Freemantle agreed with Colonel Robertson of the 35th Foot to take out French ports used as bases by privateers. In early 1813, 300 troops from Lissa were transported to the island of Lagosta (Lastovo), which had a fort and a garrison of 140 men. Captain May (35th Foot) led the storming of a battery at the foot of the fortress hill, which, with generous terms offered, led the garrison to surrender. John Hildebrand's memoirs indicate a tougher fight, including a failed first assault[24]. He was appointed to command the garrison (fifty men of 35th Foot, three hundred militia, and four gunboats), a good example of the responsibility placed on a junior officer (nineteen years old) in this theatre of operations. Leaving a garrison on Lagosta, the expeditionary force moved on to capture Port Buffalo on the island of Curzola (Korcula) with troops commanded by Major Slessor. A naval bombardment encouraged a quick surrender, as the garrison had no significant fort to retire to.

With the addition of these bases, Admiral Freemantle felt able to launch attacks on larger French ports. He moved his fleet northwards up the Dalmatian coast, capturing the island of Cherso (Cres) in May 1813 and the port of Umag in June. Fiume (Rijeka) and Rovigno (Rovinj) were the next to fall with all their shipping. This was no frigate squadron, as Freemantle had three 74-gun ships of the line, *Milford*, *Eagle* and *Elizabeth*, in addition to Hoste's *Bacchante*. At Fiume, he used the guns of his ships to pin the batteries while marines and sailors, led by Hoste and Rowley, landed to storm them from the rear. They captured ninety merchant ships in the harbour to add to their prize money. In October, Freemantle joined the Austrians (led by General Nugent of Irish birth), who had joined the allied coalition in August 1813, to capture Trieste. This was a more significant challenge than Fiume, with an imposing citadel defended by eight hundred French troops (Colonel Rabie). Freemantle provided the heavy guns the Austrians lacked; after thirteen days, the walls began to crumble, and the French surrendered. Further south, Zara (Zadar) surrendered on 6 December. All of these actions were taken on Admiral Freemantle's initiative, as he wrote to his brother, 'It is extraordinary, but since I have been in the Adriatic, not one order have I ever received relating to affairs here. This doesn't worry me in the least, because it allows me a latitude which I would not have otherwise.'[25]

Captain William Hoste wished he had a similarly distanced relationship with Freemantle, who still appears to have had proper regard for Hoste's abilities despite the fact that they did not get on. Hoste sought every opportunity for independent action, which included the usual round of intercepting French supply lines and commerce raiding. He was blockading the isolated French garrison in Cattaro, now supplied by new inland roads, when a local revolt against French rule broke out. This time the locals were split, with the Bocchese supporting the Austrians and the Montenegrins supporting Russia. Freemantle sent Hoste with money, muskets and ammunition to support the revolt.

On 13 October 1813, with his new frigate *Bacchante* (38), as well as *Saracen* (18) and three gunboats, Hoste entered the Gulf of Cattaro. General de Brigade Gauthier commanded the former Venetian fortress at Cattaro with some seven hundred Croatian and Italian troops. Although overlooked by the Montenegro mountains, it was a strongly-held position with around sixty cannons. The town and fortress of Castello Nuovo (Herzog-Novi) lie at the head of the bay, but its guns were insufficient to halt Hoste's ships. While the garrison was six hundred strong, only thirty were French, with the remainder unenthusiastic Croatian levies. On the 14th, Hoste threatened to bombard the fort while Bocchese and Montenegrin partisans assaulted from the landward side. Their fearsome reputation, coupled with the threat of naval guns, encouraged a capitulation. Both Russian and Austrian flags had to be raised to keep the insurgent factions happy! Hoste then moved down the bay to Cattaro, but could not get agreement from the insurgent factions to a viable assault plan. He did capture the island fortress of St George (Sv. Dorde) with its French gunboats. Still, even that resulted in a row with the insurgents when he wanted to remove the cannon. Each group had their own aims and did not want the British to annex the region.

Sailing back up the coast past Ragusa, which was under pressure from Austrian troops, Hoste was advised that Spalato (Split) had been abandoned, so he quickly landed and held the port until Austrian troops arrived. Meanwhile, Admiral Freemantle used British guns, the frigate *Havannah* (32), and a contingent from the 35th Foot to help the Austrians conclude the siege of Trieste. Hoste landed at Ragusa Vecchia, supporting a Ragusan noble, Count Caboga, who proclaimed the independence of Ragusa. Hoste refused to land guns to help with a siege of the city, avoiding getting involved in local politics. Finally, Hoste took a detachment of the 35th Foot and the frigate *Mermaid* to capture the last remaining French island garrison on Lesina (Hvar). Fort Napoleon is situated high above the town and harbour, and the marines found it impossible to assault without artillery, despite capturing most French officers asleep in the town. The garrison later threatened to murder the remaining officers if the commander did not capitulate. Understandably, at this stage in the war, French morale had collapsed.

Hoste then returned to Cattaro, where the sloop *Saracen* (Captain Harper) was aiding the Montenegrin siege efforts. The Montenegrins had already captured other fortifications in the Bay of Cattaro, including Budva, Trojica and Verige, with nominal British help. However, Cattaro itself needed an organised effort after demands to surrender from the British, Montenegrins and Austrians were rejected. Gauthier refused to speak to the Austrian envoy, writing in his diary that he did not want to get in touch with a 'spiv'[26]. A mutiny by Croatian troops was discovered by Gauthier, who withdrew to Fort San Giovanni (Sveti Jovan), perched on cliffs six hundred feet above sea level, reached by more than one thousand steps.

Fort San Giovanni above Cattaro (Kotor) (Author)

Hoste landed 18-pounder cannon and had them dragged up the mountain above the fort, an effort that took six days. Today, it is a steep drive on a metalled road, so to drag guns over the rocks was a considerable achievement. On Christmas Day, the British opened fire with cannons and rockets. After a six-day bombardment, fires broke out. This, coupled with the threat of a Montenegrin assault, finally persuaded the stubborn Gauthier to surrender. Hoste wrote home, 'We have got guns up mountains which were deemed impassable; and the French general said he would give me six months to get one gun up: I have convinced him of the contrary in six days… How you would laugh, were you to see me here. I am general, admiral, governor, engineer and complete jack of all trades.'[27] When the Austrians arrived, they found Cattaro occupied by the Montenegrins, and it took them a further three months to force them out. Hoste defended his decision to hand the keys to the Montenegrin Metropolitan rather than the Austrians because 'not a single Austrian soldier had ever appeared there.' He valued military contributions above all.

After leaving the Austrians to squabble with the insurgent factions, Hoste returned to Ragusa, taking eighteen cannons from Cattaro. Again, the Austrians, commanded by General Miliutinovich, were in dispute with the insurgents and astonishingly had not brought siege artillery. The 600-strong Croatian and French garrison commanded by General Montrichard were behind the walls of a strongly fortified city with 170 guns and in Fort Napoleon on a hill above the city. Their weakness was limited food supply. The insurgents had been blockading the city with assistance from a handful of British troops and gunboats from the Lagosta and Lesina garrisons[28]. The garrison had a higher regard for the insurgents than Hoste, who wrongly claimed they fled before the French. Hoste had his guns dragged up the mountains above the city on the aqueduct that provided part of the city's water supply, and then pulled them over three ridges. Ranging shots into the main square was enough to encourage surrender negotiations, and the French surrendered on 28 January[29]. The Austrians quickly marched in with Hoste's marines to forestall the return of the independent Republic of Ragusa. The historic Republic was to become a mere Austrian provincial town.

This left the great fortress of Corfu, properly five separate forts, two facing inland and three facing the sea. As the British wanted to retain the Ionian Islands, Hoste was sent to help with the siege. He took a detachment of British troops under Major Sir Charles Gordon to Parga on the mainland, where the small French garrison was persuaded to surrender. Hoste went on to Corfu, where *Bacchante* got stuck on a reef, and cannon had to be tipped overboard before the ship was light enough to work free. There was supposed to be an agreement with the French commander on Corfu to allow the British to march in, but this was delayed for a few weeks. Hoste sailed home, recovering from illness. He eventually received the recognition he sought with a baronetcy and a knighthood.

The Hundred Days campaign did not impact the naval war in the Adriatic other than a small number of engagements with French ships. The British were handing over the islands, including Lissa, to the Austrians, which was completed in July 1815. Meanwhile, the 35th Foot, the mainstay of the British army in the Adriatic, was facing the French at Waterloo.

Kingdom of Naples

On the other side of the Adriatic, Marshal Joachim Murat, Napoleon's flamboyant cavalry commander, had been named King of Naples in 1808. Murat massed twenty-five thousand troops for an invasion of Sicily. The barges were harassed by the Royal Navy, even though they were outnumbered by the French fleet. General Stuart received two new battalions and replacements, bringing his army back to strength. On 17 September 1810, four thousand Neapolitan troops crossed the Straits of Messina. While quickly engaged, the British realised this was a diversion from Murat's main attack near St Stefano. However, both landings were engaged, and the French divisional commander, General Grenier, refused to hazard his troops to support the landings. Murat returned to Naples frustrated at the lack of support. Another frustrated commander was General Stuart, who in July 1811 was replaced by Major General Lord William Cavendish-Bentinck as the army commander in the Mediterranean and envoy to the Sicilian court.

As Napoleon's armies retreated from Russia, the Russian Black Sea fleet commander Admiral Tchitchagov proposed bringing forty thousand troops to attack French territory in Dalmatia, linking up with a British invasion through Italy. Bentinck declined when he realised the cost of supplying these invasions would fall on the British. He did, however, start a series of raids on the west coast of Italy, although these could not be exploited due to domestic upheavals in Sicily. Troops also had to be detached to support Wellington's campaign in Spain.

As Napoleon retreated to France after the Battle of Leipzig (October 1813), Murat, seeing the writing on the wall, started negotiations with the Austrians to retain the Kingdom of Naples. Bentinck was sympathetic to Italian independence, having suffered the machinations of the Bourbon court in Sicily. He had, by this time, effectively taken over the island's rule. The Austrians came to an agreement with Murat to join them, which was supported by the British government, despite Bentinck's opposition. Eugene de Beauharnais resisted the Austrians in northern Italy, defeating them at Caldiero on 15 November 1813. The British force at Trieste moved with the Austrians to besiege Venice in December 1813, while Bentinck landed fourteen thousand Anglo-Sicilian troops in Italy and advanced up the east coast. It was slow going through the mountainous terrain, although largely uncontested, until they reached Genoa. He launched an attack on 17 April 1814, pushing the French back to the city. The city's defences were not strong, and a capitulation was achieved on 21 April. Bentinck took his support for Italian independence too far in northern Italy, and the British government sacked him.

Napoleon abdicated on 13 April, bringing an end to the wars that had raged for over twenty years, and the Congress of Vienna was established to reorder Europe. In Italy, Murat had control of the Kingdom of Naples, and the Austrians expected to regain control of northern Italy and the Illyrian provinces. Britain was considering what bits of the Mediterranean they wanted, and the Russians also wanted compensation. While these discussions were underway, Napoleon left his exile in Elba to begin what is known as the Hundred Days campaign, culminating in the Battle of Waterloo. Murat gambled on Napoleon and offered his services, declaring war on Austria with a plan to march forty thousand troops north and create a unified Kingdom of Italy. Two Austrian armies combined at Bologna and defeated Murat's poorly-trained army at the Battle of Tolentino on 3 May. As he retreated to Naples, Anglo-Sicilian forces were preparing to land in the south. He fled to France, where Napoleon ignored him. He later began a bizarre attempt to start an insurrection in Italy, which ended with his execution in October 1815. Arguably the final shot of the conflict.

Serbian revolt reignites

In Serbia, the Ottomans had learned none of the lessons of 1804. After the first uprising, there were attempts at reconciliation under a new governor, Süleyman Pasha. However, by 1815 repression had returned: 'Men were roasted alive, hanged by their feet over smoking straw until they asphyxiated, castrated, crushed with stones, and bastinadoed. Their women and children were raped and sometimes taken by force to harems.'[30] This resulted in the Second Serbian Uprising, led by Milos Obrenovic, starting on 23 April. He was a pig farmer, but he learned from the first uprising and avoided major military confrontations with the Ottomans. His strategy was to negotiate a deal with the Ottomans. Not that he did not raise forces and fight battles. When elected, he famously said, 'Here I am, here you are. War to the Turks!'

Milos Obrenovic (National Museum of Serbia, public domain)

There were small battles at Cacak, Ljubic, Palez and Dublje before the Ottomans were driven from the Pashalik. We don't know a great deal about these battles. They appear to have been chiefly defensive actions by the Ottomans, who defended entrenchments stormed by the Serbian forces. On several occasions, negotiated surrenders ended the action with the Ottomans withdrawing, leaving any cannon behind. The strategy was not to repeat the barbarity of the first uprising but to make a negotiated peace possible. For example, at Dublje, the Bosnian Pasha was captured after his army fled. He was treated well, given presents and allowed to return home. In mid-1815, the first negotiations began, and an agreement was reached on a form of partial autonomy. The Ottomans were wary of the Russians after Napoleon's defeat and were busy with unrest elsewhere in the empire. In 1816, formal documents acknowledged the Serbian Principality, under which they paid a yearly tax to the Porte and had a garrison of Turkish troops in Belgrade until 1867. However, it was, in most other matters, an independent state.

There was also trouble for the Ottomans in Bosnia. As in other parts of the Balkans, local leaders began to assert their independence, although in Bosnia, there was no unified leadership. In 1813, a new governor, Siliktar Ali Pasha, cracked down on dissent, subduing revolts in Sarajevo and Mostar.

CHAPTER SIX

ARMED FORCES IN THE ADRIATIC

There are many excellent studies of Napoleonic armies and their uniforms, organisation and tactics. So, in this chapter, we will focus on the units that served in the Adriatic.

France

Before the Napoleonic Wars, the French army had suffered from many of the problems facing French society as a whole. For example, only nobles typically were promoted above the rank of captain, with less than one-third actually serving with their regiments. Unsurprisingly, republican sentiments were strong in the army, although the purges, emigration and massive expansion initially damaged it, more so in the cavalry than in technical arms like the artillery.

The main French army facing the Austrian territories in the Adriatic was the Armée d'Italie, not to be confused with the Army of the Kingdom of Italy. In 1806 this army included 50,430 French troops and 6,510 Italian troops. By 1809, prior to the war against Austria, that army had grown to 77,543 French and 28,285 Italian troops. French troops were sent to fight in the Adriatic land campaigns, although locally-raised and Italian units became increasingly important. By this time, the term 'regiment' had been reinstated, replacing the demi-brigade of the revolutionary wars. There were Line and Light (Légère) regiments, although the practical differences became less important over time. In 1805 regiments had three battalions (one a depot unit). Each field battalion had one grenadier, one voltigeur and seven fusilier companies. The book strength of a company was 123 men, although, in practice, 80 was typical, giving a battalion strength of 720.

In 1807, the infantry regiments started to reorganise into four field battalions and one depot battalion. Each field battalion was reduced from seven to four fusilier companies, with company strength remaining unchanged. French regiments included troops recruited from areas annexed to France, such as parts of Italy and Belgium. With some variations, this remained the core infantry organisation for the rest of the war. There were also guard and cavalry regiments, but these did not play a significant role in the Adriatic campaigns. Field artillery batteries were attached to infantry divisions and typically included six field pieces (8-pdr) and two howitzers (5.5"). Heavy batteries (12-pdr) were attached to the corps, which would have been rare in the Adriatic. In 1812, infantry regiments were assigned two 3-pdr guns, which probably did not reach the Adriatic units. The classic infantry jacket was blue, becoming shorter by 1812. The bicorn was replaced by the shako in 1806, becoming slightly taller from 1810. Breeches were white with black gaiters, although white, grey or buff overalls were often worn on campaign.

French line infantry 1807 (General Research Division,
The New York Public Library. [1910]. France, 1807)

In 1806, the Austrian territories ceded to France after Austerlitz were incorporated into the Kingdom of Italy. The Army of the Kingdom of Italy[1] broadly followed French organisation, with green jackets in 1805, changing to white in 1808. In addition, the Kingdom raised local units in the new territories, including the Royal Dalmatian Legion/Regiment and the short-lived Istrian Light Infantry Battalion.

French and Italian units serving in Illyria included General Molitor's division, which occupied the territories in 1806 and consisted of the 5th, 23rd, 79th and 81st Line regiments. When the Russians attacked in 1806, additional troops were sent: 18th Light, 11th and 60th Line, 24th Chasseurs à cheval and five artillery companies. In addition, the Kingdom of Italy provided two battalions of the Royal Guard, two artillery companies and the Bersaglieri di Brescia.

These units were formed into Marmont's Army of Dalmatia for the 1809 campaign against Austria. Organised into two divisions under Montrichard and Clausel, they fought across Croatia and joined Napoleon in Vienna. They returned to Dalmatia after this campaign but were reduced to one division in 1811 because troops were needed in Spain and then Russia. By 1813 only the 79th Line regiment was left in Dalmatia. The Corfu garrison was augmented by the 14th Light and 6th Line regiments and a few troops of the 25th Chasseurs à cheval.

French foot artillery (General Research Division, The New York Public Library. [1910]. France 1806)

In 1809, these territories, along with the rest of the coastline ceded by Austria, were reorganised into the Illyrian Provinces, an autonomous province of France. French regiments served there as above, but these were supplemented by locally-raised units. Foreign regiments were not a revolutionary invention; they had a long tradition in the French army. After 1809 around one-third of the Grande Armée was foreign; by 1812, more than half was. As John Elting puts it, 'The French, being a thrifty and practical people, have always been eager to let any available foreigners assist them in any necessary bleeding and dying for *la Patrie*.'[2] In the Adriatic, these included:

Royal Dalmatian Regiment: This was a four-battalion regiment created from previous Dalmatian battalions. It was stationed across the region, with the 1st in Italy, 2nd in Venice, and the other two garrisoning Zadar, Ragusa and Cattaro. An artillery battery was attached in 1809. In 1812, three battalions joined the Grande Armée in Russia, and the survivors reformed in Venice before being rebuilt and stationed across Dalmatia. They wore a green tunic with red facings, green trousers and a black Austrian-style *corsehut* cap, replaced by a shako in 1808. Battalions had the typical French strength of around 720 men.

Royal Istrian Battalion: A single battalion that struggled to recruit to its full strength, it served in coastal garrisons on the Istrian coast. Its members wore a green tunic with sky-blue facings, grey trousers, black boots and the black corsehut, replaced by the shako in 1808.

Pandours: The French raised several units (around 1810) using the traditional name for Balkan irregulars, including the Dalmatian Pandours, Pandours of Cattaro, and Albanian Pandours. They carried out policing duties inland and guarded the Ottoman border. While receiving no pay, they had plunder rights in wartime. The uniforms and weapons were of local origin. Typically, the uniform was a red turban, waistcoat and dolman over a white shirt, and blue trousers with a white (red for NCOs) cloak. Weapons included the long Balkan musket, knives and pistols.

Croat regiments: Sometimes called Chasseurs Illyrians, these were the former Austrian Grenze regiments living in the part of the Military Border ceded to France. They retained their Austrian numbering and organisation of two battalions of six companies, expanding to four battalions in wartime. They also had a small light artillery detachment. In 1810, the total force totalled 18,197. While Napoleon was persuaded to keep their traditional structure, he abolished the 'honorary exemption' that had previously sheltered most of the middle class from military service[3]. They served on border duty, in garrisons along the coast, and by fighting Ottoman and Montenegrin raiders. For field service, troops were taken from these regiments to create four Croatian provisional regiments. The 1st and 3rd Regiments served in the Russian campaign and in Germany. The 2nd Regiment also served in Germany. Four Croatian battalions, plus two French, also took part in Marshal Marmont's punitive expedition into Ottoman Bosnia in May 1810.

Various attempts were made to change the Austrian uniform, but most troops retained the brown tunic with light blue trousers. The 1810 regulations included a blue tunic, but it is unclear how many were actually issued. The 3rd Regiment was issued with green tunics and trousers with yellow facings and a shako. The 2nd Regiment retained its brown uniforms. The French also continued the Austrian practice of attaching two hundred Serezaners to act as scouts and couriers; they wore traditional local dress rather than a uniform, often distinguished by a red hooded cloak.

Illyrian Regiment: This unit was raised in 1810 from non-frontier areas (Carniola and Carinthia) of the newly acquired territories. Its four battalions served in the Russian campaign, and the battalion-strength survivors in the 1813 campaign in Germany. They were issued French light infantry uniforms, distinguished as a foreign regiment by 'swallow's nest' shoulder wings.

Illyrian Chasseur 1810 (General Research Division, The
New York Public Library. [1910]. France, 1807)

Croatian Hussar Regiment: Established in February 1813 from border units, it was organised on the French hussar model of six squadrons and was based at Karlstadt (Karlovac). It was meant to serve in Germany, but was not equipped in time. However, 220 Hussars did take part in a successful operation to repulse an Ottoman raid, although they had a mixture of equipment, including medieval halberds! The unit was later sent to Italy, but was deemed to be unreliable.

Garde Nationale: These were raised from the local population in coastal towns, numbering ten thousand men by 1811. They included coastal gun batteries. The wealthy paid for French-style uniforms, but most troops wore civilian dress. They were provided with weapons, but were only paid when serving away from their home towns. Performance was mixed; they occasionally repelled British raids, but more often scattered during combat.

In the Ionian Islands, several local units were raised to garrison the islands and the mainland ports. These included the following:

Albanian Regiment: Most members of this regiment were refugees from Ali Pasha's rule, continued the Venetian and Russian militia traditions. In 1809, it was reorganised into six (some sources say five) battalions totalling 160 officers and 2,934 men by Colonel Minot. Discipline was relaxed as all were volunteers, and combat performance was mixed. The British ambassador reported that the French failure to pay them regularly encouraged desertion to Ali Pasha[4]. They wore their local Albanian-style costume, equipped with the long Balkan musket, pistols, and a *yataghan* sword.

Oriental Chasseurs: This was an understrength battalion, originally raised in the Middle East and attached to the Albanian Regiment after serving in General Molitor's relief expedition to the siege of Ragusa in 1806.

Septinsular Battalion: This was raised from a former Venetian regiment that had also been in Russian pay. The establishment was nine companies of one hundred men. However, recruitment difficulties meant the ranks were topped up with Austrian prisoners and others from outside the islands. After the detachment on Cephalonia (Colonel Piéris) surrendered to the British without firing a shot in 1809, Napoleon decided the battalion was not worth the cost, and it was disbanded in 1812. It wore the French dark blue light infantry uniform.

Ionian Mounted Chasseurs: This was a single company (128 men) of light cavalry, recruited locally, and supplemented by men of the 25th Chasseurs à cheval from the Kingdom of Naples. They adopted that regiment's uniform of a green jacket with red facings. Other small units of pioneers and gendarmes were probably dressed in civilian clothing.

Septinsular Artillery: Two companies, who wore the same uniforms as French foot artillery of the line.

Foreign regiments raised elsewhere in the empire could also serve in the Adriatic. The Isenburg (Isembourg), named '2. Imperial French Foreign Regiment', is one example; part of it served for a period in the Corfu garrison. The rank and file were primarily recruited from Austrian prisoners of war captured at Ulm.

French Navy in the Adriatic

The French navy turned out to be the less effective element of Napoleon's military strength, for a variety of reasons. The revolution deprived the navy of many of its most competent officers, and although French ships were at least as good as those of their enemies, its sailors never managed to match the skill of their primary opponent, the Royal Navy. It was also a matter of priorities. France was primarily a continental military power, while Britain was a maritime power. Napoleon had little interest or understanding of naval operations, occasionally with disastrous results. The French had no marines as such. The four marine infantry regiments that were created in 1792 were used as garrisons for ports. The Artillerie de Marine (twelve battalions in 1803) did, on occasion, fight at sea, but they were mainly used on land. Even sailors could be redeployed for use on land, mainly as engineers. One small advantage the French navy did have was its own unique signalling system, which John Paul Jones considered far superior to the British system of flag signals.

The Adriatic French fleet, including ships from the Kingdom of Italy, inherited a modest number of outdated Venetian ships and other small vessels from the Italian states. These included galleys and xebecs whose oars could, on occasion, save the day. The fleet also acquired former Austrian ships (two galleys, two brigs, ten gunboats and smaller vessels), establishing the Illyrian Flotilla, which guarded harbours and escorted coastal convoys. On 18 February 1806, the Russian frigate *Venus* engaged a galley near Fiume, catching it quickly downwind. Still, when the galley changed direction, the Russian ship foundered. The galley could retreat to shallow water where the frigate could not follow. They also used xebecs, formally or as privateers, which raided as far south as Preveza. On 3 July 1806, *Venus* came across 11 French xebecs and gunboats in the sandy shallows of Cape Gomena (Lovište), opposite Korcula. *Venus* gave chase and got within the range of cannon shot when the wind dropped. The French flotilla furled their sails and rowed away, much to the Russians' frustration.

In 1810 Napoleon appointed Bernard Dubourdieu to command his Adriatic forces. His appointment came with instructions to keep the British out of the Adriatic, utilizing a squadron of five frigates and three brigs, as well as liaising with the French director of the Venice Arsenale (Tupinier) over the construction of ships of the line. In 1808 as many as five ships of the line were on the stocks in Venice, but they took a long time to build, not helped by the Royal Navy disrupting supplies of timber from Croatia.

Dubourdieu, whose attempts to capture Lissa are covered above, had more challenges than building serviceable ships. His crews were a mixture of French and Venetian professional seamen and Italian and Slav conscripts. By 1811, the French Navy was short of sailors, exacerbated by the practice of diverting personnel to the army. An extraordinary levy took four hundred men from Corsica and two hundred from the Ionian Islands. Adriatic crews had seen little action, and it would take a lot of training and time to get them close to the level of expertise of a Royal Navy squadron. The French claimed few Italian officers handled ships with daring and skill, and their sailors never mastered the more complicated ship handling required for frigates. Patience was not a virtue Napoleon was known for!

Russia

The regular Russian army was established by Peter the Great, but it was under Catherine the Great that Russia was recognised as a major European power. With over forty million people to draw from, the Russian army was rarely short of manpower. At the outset of the Napoleonic Wars, it had 50 regiments of cavalry and 208 battalions of infantry. The rank and file were conscripted from serfs tied to the land, serving for twenty-five years. Western observers admired their stoicism, if not their plundering. Officers were recruited from the minor gentry, generally regarded as the worst educated in Europe, some of which reached high ranks. One contemporary observer described General Lacy, Russian commander in chief in the Mediterranean, thus: 'He had been, no doubt, a brave and meritorious officer: but he was now between seventy and eighty years of age, and showed no trace of ever having been a man of talent or information.... At the councils of war...he used to bring his nightcap in his pocket, put it on, and go to sleep while others discussed the business.'[5]

Under Tsar Alexander I, army reforms brought new uniforms and tactics, and observers admired the progress being made with better armed and equipped soldiers, even if supply issues and the disregard for the well-being of the ordinary soldier remained. In 1805 Vice Admiral Dmitriy Nikolayevich Senyavin was appointed to command naval and land forces in the Mediterranean at a relatively youthful forty-two years of age. As we have seen, he and his forces performed well on sea and land, only to have his efforts undone by the Peace of Tilsit.

Before 1806 there was no higher organisational unit than regiments, which were grouped into regional 'inspections'. This chaotic system was reformed in 1806-8 with the introduction of divisions, typically with two musketeer and one Jager brigade of two regiments each. There were seventy-seven musketeer regiments, thirteen of grenadiers and twenty of Jagers. The regimental establishment was 2,256, with 1,385 for Jagers. Tactics emphasised the use of the bayonet, with Prince Bagration declaring in 1812 that 'the cannon-ball is a foolish virgin and the bayonet a wise virgin.' While ostensibly light infantry, the Jagers were, in practice, little different from the musketeer regiments, as there was no light infantry manual until 1818. There was a little more emphasis on marksmanship, and morale appears to have been higher. The army was reformed again in 1811, introducing the corps system, but these reforms had little impact on our story.

In 1806, the 15th Division under Major General Heinrich Reinhold was the main army unit in the Adriatic, constituting the original forces under Lacy, less the Siberian Grenadiers and Aleksopol Musketeer regiments that had returned to Russia[6]. This division consisted of the Kura, Kozlov, Kolyvan and Vitebsk Musketeer regiments (three battalions each), 13th and 14th Jagers (three battalions each) and three position artillery companies of the 6th Artillery regiment (twelve 12-pdrs each). There was also a Corfu garrison battalion and a locally-raised light infantry legion recruited mainly from Greeks. The numbers varied, reaching a peak of 2,340 in 1807.

The infantry uniform was modernised in 1801, although there would have been significant delays in implementation. The infantry jacket was dark green with facing colours that reflected the 'inspection'. Shoulder straps were coloured according to the seniority of the regiment. White breeches were worn with black shoes in summer and below-the-knee black boots in winter. Musketeers had a black bicorne hat, grenadiers a mitre cap; both were replaced by a shako from 1805, although officers retained the bicorne. In the Adriatic, the Kozlov Musketeer Regiment had dark green collars and cuffs, with lilac cuffs before 1805 and red afterwards. The shoulder straps were turquoise, and the hat pompon centre was grey. The Kolyvan Musketeer regiment had raspberry collars and cuffs, yellow shoulder straps and a pink pompon centre. The Vitebsk Musketeer regiment had light ochre collar and cuffs, raspberry shoulder straps, and a white pompon centre. Jager uniforms were similar to those of musketeer regiments, although the regiments serving in the Adriatic probably had the earlier light green jacket. Green breeches were worn in winter, and the shako had a pronounced brim. The 13th Jagers had collar, cuffs and pompon in light ochre, while the 14th Jagers had the same in maroon (chestnut). As with all Napoleonic uniforms, colours are approximate and could vary with wear and tear. Artillery wore infantry-style uniforms with black facings and red piping. The army also had Guards, Cossacks and cavalry regiments, but these did not serve in the Adriatic. In 1807, facing colours were all red. Numbered shoulder straps to distinguish units, and a new shako, were introduced in 1809. However, the Russians had left the Adriatic before these reforms were introduced. Russian regulations required the rank and file to wear ties at all times. This was unpopular, particularly in bad weather. In the 1809 campaign in Bulgaria, Prince Bagration abandoned this requirement, increasing his popularity with the troops[7]. Russian muskets had little standardisation, with twenty-eight different calibres by 1812. English muskets were also issued as rewards, adding to the variety.

For the Russo-Turkish War of 1806-12, Tsar Alexander created the Russian Army of the Dniester, commanded by General Michelson. It consisted of two corps with ninety infantry battalions, one hundred squadrons of regular cavalry, eight Cossack regiments, and 286 guns. The 1st Corps of two divisions was commanded by Essen, and the 2nd Corps of three divisions was commanded by Meyendorff. We have covered the main actions in the narrative as they impacted the war in the Adriatic.

As with other navies, the Russians used sailors as landing parties in amphibious operations. In addition, there were marines or naval infantry. They were organised into four regiments, three attached to the Baltic Fleet and one to the Black Sea Fleet, as well as one independent battalion in the Caspian Sea. In the Mediterranean, they deployed four companies of the 1st Regiment, two of the 2nd, four of the 3rd, and four of the 4th—fourteen companies. In November 1806, the ten companies from the Baltic Fleet regiments were consolidated into the 2nd Naval Infantry Regiment (Colonel Boissel)[8]. Naval infantry followed army organisation and ranks. The uniform of naval infantry was the same as that of the musketeer regiments.

Britain

The British army of the Napoleonic Wars was relatively small, with only forty thousand men in 1793. However, it grew to two hundred and fifty thousand by 1813, with the largest force being deployed in the Peninsular War under the command of the Duke of Wellington. As an institution, the army was not popular, and the rank and file were drawn mainly from those who had little choice—in Wellington's famous words, 'The scum of the earth'. The second part of the quote, 'It is really wonderful that we should have made them to the fine fellows they are', is less well-known, and is a claim justified by the army's later performance as the only army not to have suffered a major reverse at the hands of Napoleonic France. While commissions could be purchased, later reforms relaxed the requirements. They became more by seniority, although promotion by merit was rare and advancement from the ranks even rarer.

The main British army in the Mediterranean was based in Sicily. In March 1805, General Sir James Craig was appointed commander of British land forces in the Mediterranean, with General Sir John Stuart as his second in command. Stuart took command in 1806 when Craig became ill. He was replaced by Generals Fox and Moore after his victory at Maida, but returned in 1808. His orders were to ensure the island did not fall to the French, even if that meant going against their ally King Ferdinand. Like other commanders in this theatre, he had significant discretion, given that it could take ten weeks to get a message to London and the same in return. He went there with four thousand men, a tiny force by the standards of the Napoleonic Wars. The Russians had sent eleven thousand men to the Ionian Islands, and Archduke Charles had ninety thousand men in northern Italy. Messina became the main base of the British army, where an invasion from the mainland could be resisted.

The British foot regiments had varied experience. The 20th, 27th and 35th Foot had experience in Europe or in the Egyptian campaign. However, the 58th, 61st, 78th and 81st Foot were all inexperienced, particularly the 78th, a Highland regiment transferred from Malta, which Stuart called 'a corps of boys'. He also had around thirty-five hundred Sicilian regulars and a militia which he described as 'altogether an illusion—without arms, without system, without organisation, and without pay, it is a mere list of names.'[9] As we have seen, the British also had the Royal Navy, which meant that fairly small forces could be inserted almost anywhere on the long coastline held by the French. As Joseph Bonaparte wrote to Napoleon, 'Eight thousand men in English ships is the equivalent to fifty thousand men here, as in eight days, they can be transported to eight different places.'[10]

Royal Marine (General Research Division, The New York Public Library. [1910]. Great Britain, 1813-15)

The British army supplemented its lack of troops by recruiting foreign regiments. As late as 1813, one in eight men was a foreigner. In Sicily, this included a battalion of de Watteville's Swiss regiment, detachments of the Royal Corsican Rangers, Royal Sicilian Volunteers and the Chasseurs Britanniques. The British army was always short of cavalry, and only one squadron of the 20th Light Dragoons was at Stuart's disposal. Despite these limitations, the army performed well at Maida, demonstrating the worth of disciplined musketry. An experimental light battalion formed from the light companies of the line regiments was also effective.

The 1st Battalion of the 35th (Sussex) Foot was the only British regiment to play a significant role in the Adriatic. It was an experienced unit that had fought in the West Indies and Flanders before joining the expeditionary force to Sicily in 1805. It distinguished itself at the Battle of Maida, capturing the French General Louis Compère. The battalion suffered significant casualties during the 1807 Alexandria expedition, and returned to Sicily to recuperate. As we have seen, elements of the 35th Foot took part in garrisons and offensive operations in conjunction with the navy, a level of cooperation that was not always achieved elsewhere during the Napoleonic Wars. Recruitment to the 35th Foot was challenging, perhaps due to overseas service. The regimental history notes that in 1810, 'The difficulty of obtaining recruits in England about this time caused the bounty to rise to the large sum of forty pounds.'[11] By the end of the Napoleonic Wars, the regiment had spent so much time in the Ionian Islands that they had children with local women who spoke Italian and Greek fluently; they also had, in the words of a British traveller, 'acquired much adaptation to the manners of the south of Europe', with service 'easy, even luxurious; the climate fine; provisions, wine, fruits, extremely cheap; and much goodwill existing between soldiers and the natives.'[12] The regiment would have worn the standard line infantry uniform with orange facings that reflected the regiment's earlier association with King William's House of Orange.

The two flank companies of the 44th (East Essex) Foot, part of the Malta garrison, also took part in the 1809 Adriatic operations. This was the 1st Battalion that had served in the Egyptian campaign in 1801 before going home and then returning to the Mediterranean in May 1805. Later on, they were part of the British force that burnt the White House in Washington during the War of 1812 with the United States. The regiment would have worn the standard line infantry uniform with yellow facings.

Britain had not traditionally recruited large numbers of foreign troops within its formal establishment. There had been ad hoc recruitment during conflicts, such as German troops during the American Revolution, and the 60th (Royal American) had become something of a depository of foreign troops, mainly Swiss and Germans. The French Revolution changed official policy, and several units were raised from Royalist émigrés, rising to about eighteen per cent of the army in 1808. These provided an important source of troops for overseas commitments, like the Adriatic, given the modest size of the British army. The foreign auxiliary corps were often officered by noblemen displaced from their homes and were frequently older than their equivalents in the British Army. An ensign of forty years of age was not unusual. Desertion to the enemy of the rank and file was not unheard of, and Napoleon's amnesty for émigrés that had not served as officers in foreign armies encouraged many to return to France.

Several units were proposed, but not all lasted for long. For example, **Broderick's Regiment** was to be raised from Albanians in 1799. While some recruits assembled in Corfu, the unit was later abandoned. There was a similar story for a unit of Albanians due to be raised by Colonel Villettes in the same year. Nevertheless, the following units played a role in the Adriatic at some stage during the conflict.

The **Chasseurs Britanniques** was formed in 1801 as a light infantry battalion of six companies totalling around six hundred men. They embarked from Trieste with German, Polish and Swiss troops, officered by French émigrés. They saw limited action in the 1801 Egyptian campaign and went to garrison Malta until 1803. Then the light and grenadier companies were sent as reinforcements for the assault on Santa Maura, although it appears they were held in reserve. After that, they went back to Sicily and then fought in the Peninsular War. They wore a green coatee with yellow facings, grey breeches and black half-gaiters.

The brief occupation of Corsica resulted in the recruitment of several small units. The **Corsican Rangers** was raised in Minorca from Corsican refugees and, under the command of Major Hudson Lowe, performed well in the Egyptian campaign as light infantry. It was disbanded in 1802 following the Treaty of Amiens. Its members wore a green jacket with black facings, sky blue breeches and a black shako. Hudson Lowe then raised the **Royal Corsican Rangers** in Malta in September 1803. They fought at Maida and became part of the Sicily garrison. Two companies took part in the Ionian Islands campaign in 1809-1810. In 1811 they were expanded to twelve companies and posted to the Ionian Islands, with detachments at Lissa from 1812. From there, they took part in the capture of Lagosta (Lastovo), Curzola (Korcula), and finally, Trieste and Ragusa (Dubrovnik) in 1813. The uniform appears to have been rifle green with scarlet facings, although they may have received red jackets in 1813.

Hudson Lowe, Royal Corsican Rangers (Seaton, R. C. [Robert Cooper], 1853-1915, public domain)

Proposals to create a Croat regiment were rejected, but two independent companies were raised and attached to the Royal Corsican Rangers to garrison Curzola. Some Croatian militia in French service deserted in 1812 and made their way to Lissa. Colonel Robertson gained permission to form a corps from these men to be known as the '**Illyrian Light Infantry**', but it does not seem to have grown into much of a unit. Robertson soon found it easier to supply passage for these deserters to join the Austrian Army under General Nugent in northern Italy.

Dillon's Regiment (Edward's, not Henry's, which served in the West Indies) was raised in Italy in 1795. It had French émigré officers, with men recruited from Germany and the Balkans from 1796. It had two battalions that fought in most Mediterranean actions before joining the Malta garrison in 1802. It moved to Sicily in 1808, and elements briefly fought in the Adriatic. They wore a red coatee with yellow facings, a white waistcoat and breeches, and later probably grey trousers.

Meuron's Regiment was a Swiss regiment in British pay. It was raised in India and sent to the Mediterranean in 1807, serving in Gibraltar, Sicily and

Malta. Detachments are mentioned as serving in the Ionian Islands campaign. They wore the standard British uniform with sky blue facings.

Roll's Regiment was another Swiss unit; raised in 1794, it served in the Egyptian campaign, then in garrison duty in Gibraltar and Sicily. It was augmented by four hundred Swiss in French service who were captured in Portugal in 1809. Two companies played a role in the attack on Santa Maura in 1810. In 1812, two companies went to the Ionian Islands. Their uniform was broadly the standard British one with royal blue facings from 1805.

De Roll's Regiment (Henri Garnier [aka Tanconville], public domain)

The **Calabrian Free Corps** was raised as light infantry in 1809 from Italian refugees, with a staff of British officers. They fought at Santa Maura in 1810, and six companies remained in the Ionian Islands. Two companies participated in the siege of Trieste in October 1813. Lord Bentinck regarded them as perhaps the best light infantry in the Mediterranean, despite some 'low bred, bad Calabrese officers.'[13] They wore a blue jacket with green (some had blue) trousers, black gaiters, and a black cylindrical light infantry shako.

The **Greek Light Infantry** was raised by Captain Richard Church in the Ionian Islands in March 1810. A second regiment was raised in June 1813. It took part in the capture of Santa Maura and then garrisoned Zante. Finally, it was sent to Montenegro in June 1812 to quell a revolt. In his memoirs John Hildebrand (35th Foot) was scathing about this unit: 'The 1st Battalion of the Greek Light Infantry Corps was raised, a fine looking body of men but, as it turned out, utterly useless as soldiers and worse; so troublesome and unruly in discipline that, however hard the duties of the different garrisons of Zante, Santa Maura, Cephalonia, &c, no commanding officer could ever be persuaded to have that corps, if he could possibly avoid it; and as, after the addition of a 2nd Battalion (actually the 2nd Regiment), it formed a force of two thousand men, it was not only a large and useless expense to the country, but by filling up the place of a more desirable reinforcement, was a constant and vexatious annoyance.'[14] This appears to be a harsh view, as the regiment fought well at the siege of Santa Maura. Its officers (seventy-five per cent Greek or Albanians, the rest British) included Theodoros Kolokotronis, then a major but later a Greek general and the preeminent leader of the Greek War of Independence (1821-1829). However, the regiment was described as being in a 'very indifferent state' by 1813. The uniform was probably the most exotic of the foreign regiments serving in the Adriatic, being 'in the Albanian fashion'. The jacket was red with yellow facings, and was worn with a white fustanella (Greek kilt) and stockings.

In October 1809, the **Ionian Islands Volunteer Militias** were established on all the islands after the British conquest. By 1810 this was reported to have grown to some four thousand men armed at their own expense.

The **Italian Levy or regiments** were established from Italian prisoners of war. They appear to have had a mixed record, serving in Sicily and the Peninsular War. A detachment from the 1st Regiment took part in the siege of Trieste in October 1813. They wore a blue jacket with red facings, and blue trousers.

To give an idea of how detachments from regiments, and foreign officers, were used in the Adriatic, we can look at the initial garrison of Lissa in May 1812. In the Monthly Returns for the 35th Foot, the following are stated to be on Lissa: Major John Herries, Captains Francis May and Thomas King, Lieutenants Archibald McDonald and Richard Webb, Ensign John Hildebrand, Assistant Surgeon John Ludlow. Eight sergeants, two drummers, two hundred rank and file. Royal Artillery 1st Lieutenant William Rains with a detachment of thirty men. In the Monthly Returns for the Corsican Rangers, the following are on Lissa: Captains Gerolame and Pearce Lowen, Lieutenant Cosmo Gugliano, and Ensigns Perette and Rigo with two hundred soldiers. De Roll's Regiment had Captain Joseph Barbier and Lieutenant Otto Salinger with two hundred rank and file. Calabrian Free Corps had Captain Roncus with one hundred soldiers.

Ottoman Empire

The Ottomans were the dominant military power in the Balkans in the 17th century, but they were increasingly vulnerable in the 18th century. Large armies did not mask the failure to introduce civil and military reforms. George Koehler, a German in British service who spent six months observing the Ottoman war machine, reported, 'Their resources are no doubt very great as to men, money and all kind of military stores etc. But the vices of their government, and total ignorance in the art of war, renders it next to impossible that they should be able by their own efforts to maintain their independence.'[15]

The main field army rarely engaged in the Adriatic campaigns, leaving the borders to the Ottoman governors and the provincial *ayans*. Ottoman armies were unlike any other Napoleonic-era army, not just in troop types but also in command, organisation and discipline. Western observers were generally scathing about Ottoman generals and noted that units fought as individuals rather than as organised battalions. This partly reflects the smaller number of officers and trained NCOs. The Nizam-I-Cedit (New Order Army) was an attempt to introduce a western-style organisation, but even here, there was a shortage of officers. In 1799 there was one officer per 93 men, falling to one officer per 343 men in 1801. Cavalry had once been the cutting edge of Ottoman armies, but by this period they could rarely engage with Western regular infantry successfully. They also failed to coordinate infantry, cavalry and artillery as the European armies did.

The Kapikulu Army was the permanent standing army. The Janissary Corps was the main infantry element of this force, organised into four divisions comprised of *ortas* of varying strength. There were 229 ortas, with 77 based in Istanbul and the remainder at critical points across the empire. There were vast numbers of janissaries on paper, but a 1798 survey recorded 113,400 as being active military. The Cannon Corps (Topcu Ocagi) both manufactured artillery and served the guns on campaign. In siege warfare, they were supported by the Miners (Lagimciyan) and the Mortar Men (Humbarciyan). The regular cavalry was the Kapikulu Suvarileri, organised into six divisions; on paper it was around twenty-eight thousand strong, but in practice, some ten thousand were militarily active.

By the 18th century, provincial forces included an armed militia (*levend*) that formed the bulk of Ottoman infantry forces. There are many names attributed to provincial units, but Sekban battalions could be hired for campaigns or be part of a long-term force. Arnauts were paid units, usually Albanians, although the name is often ascribed to others; they were regarded as some of the better Ottoman troops. Albanian troops in the Ottoman armies were typically organised into 'battalions' of two to three hundred men, commanded by a *serçesme* (sergeant major) who was proposed by the men and approved by the ayan. They would usually go home during the winter, unless they were serving outside the Balkans.

Arnaut soldier (General Research Division, The New York Public Library. [1910]. Turkey, 1810-17.)

Derbents, known as Martolos in Greece, were primarily local defence militias but could see action in field armies. The main cavalry units were the sipahi, traditionally granted timars (fiefs) by the Sultan. They brought their own weapons and armour, accompanied by their armed retainers. However, the sipahi were rarely armoured by this period, and light cavalry could be provided by the *deli* (madmen), who are still reported as being in service in our period. Bosnia provided significant numbers of light cavalry in troops of between twenty and fifty men, called *faris*. The loss of the Tatar Khanate to Russia in 1783 removed the major source of irregular light cavalry.

Selim III made some efforts to reform the military, building on his father's reforms. The basic principle was to separate the administrative from the military functions of each corps. Barracks were modernised, regular drills introduced, and in return, wages were paid monthly. The janissary rolls were halved to about thirty thousand men, and the sons of members were only allowed to join if they had ability. However, reforms to the janissaries and sipahi were only partly successful, with abuses hidden from inspectors. They were more successful in the artillery after the arrival of the French General Aubert du Bayet as ambassador in 1796. He helped develop foundries and technical schools.

The most radical reform was the creation of the Nizam-i-Cedit, or New Order Army, organised, trained and clothed in the European manner. Its barracks were established outside Istanbul, away from the gaze of the janissaries, and its personnel recruited mainly from Anatolian peasant boys. The corps grew from 2,536 men and 27 officers in May 1797 to 9,263 men and 27 officers in July 1801. After conscription was introduced in 1802, the corps grew to 22,685 men and 1,590 officers by the end of 1806[16]. Each regiment had twelve companies (Boluks) with an establishment of eighty-eight officers and twelve hundred men, plus attached light artillery and support troops[17]. By the end of Selim's reign, observers praised their efficiency, although attempts to expand the system into the Balkans were resisted by local governors. With the overthrow of Selim, the corps was disbanded, and the janissaries killed every officer they could find. However, units outside the capital survived and formed the basis of a new army when Sultan Mahmud destroyed the janissaries in 1826.

Nizam-i-Cedit Infantry. (General Research Division, The New York Public Library. [1910]. Turkey, 1810-17.)

Ayans like Ali Pasha could field large armies that reflected the nature of wars in the Balkans. Estimates vary from the British ambassador to the Porte's three hundred thousand to a more realistic sixteen thousand by Major Leake, who was on the ground training his troops. During wartime, Ali could field up to fifty thousand men, mostly drawn from his Albanian subjects (Skipetars), including his own janissaries. They were mainly Muslim, but he had Greek Orthodox troops and a Catholic battalion called the Mirdites from northern Albania. He also recruited from further afield, including a unit of one hundred Tartar cavalry.

The terrain in Epirus did not lend itself to the regimented armies of the western powers. Ali was impressed by the discipline of the janissaries, when he campaigned with the main Ottoman army, but recognised they were a declining force. He was interested in western military science and accepted assistance, equipment and training from the French and the British. Using this expertise, he increased the use of artillery and improved the defences of his forts. This included six hundred Congreve rockets from the British, which he used in the siege of Berat. They were notoriously inaccurate but had a demoralising effect on the enemy's morale. However, warfare remained sporadic, and his troops were often reluctant to make direct assaults. His capital at Ioannina had a permanent garrison of three thousand men, twenty-nine cannons (12- and 24-pounders) and five mortars.

Albanian soldier (General Research Division, The New York Public Library. [1910]. Turkey, 1810-17.)

Ottoman uniforms are a complex and disputed subject. Fortunately, there is an excellent book by Chris Flaherty that brings together the available evidence with colour plates[18].

The Ottoman Navy

The Ottoman Empire possessed a significant navy, despite its destruction at the Battle of Chesma (1770) during the Russo-Turkish War. Sultan Selim inherited a rebuilding programme, which used modern British and French designs to construct a fleet of twenty-two ships of the line (called Kalyon), fifteen frigates and many smaller ships. This was a blue-water navy that also had gunboats to operate on the great rivers of the empire. Selim appointed Kucuk Huseyin as Kapitan Pasha and attracted overseas officers and technicians, reintroducing conscription and tackling corruption. The British ambassador reported in 1787 that they had twenty-six ships of the line with six more on the stocks, twenty-four frigates, and forty sloops.[19] By 1800, the fleet had thirty ships of the line and fifty frigates and brigs. The otherwise critical military mission to the Porte was pretty complimentary about reforms to the Ottoman navy[20]. However, the war against Russia resulted in funds being diverted to the army, and the navy again declined. Sultan Mahmud came to the throne in 1808 and strengthened the navy so it could once again challenge the Russians in the Black Sea.

The newer Ottoman ships were mostly of French design, with more traditional eastern designs used for coastal and river warfare, including oar-powered galleys. In 1799 the flagship, *Sultan Selim*, mounted one hundred and twenty 42-pounders and at least ten more of smaller calibre, with a crew of fourteen hundred men. However, in western and Russian navies, the number of gun ports usually equalled the number of guns, which was not always the case in the Ottoman Navy. This was probably because of the earlier light single-frame hulls, the use of expensive bronze cannons, and the way the Ottomans deployed their ships[21].

The reforms included a naval academy and a system of ranks based more on ability than bribery. Sailors mainly came from the Ottoman Empire's Greek subjects, who were as good as any in the world. However, the weakness of the officer corps made fleet manoeuvre difficult, so the Ottomans chose to defend inlets, swinging their ships on the anchor chains. This tactic also reflected the shorter range of guns and large crews and the subservience of the navy to army operations. Fleets were often supplemented by large numbers of oared gunboats. Marines were provided by the 31st Orta of Janissaries, augmented by two units of naval riflemen known as Galangis. Other janissary units also had naval insignia, including the 88th, 8th Boluk and 56th Cemaat ortas. It is possible that these primarily served on river flotillas. The ship's captain was the Rais, assisted by junior officers known as Mulazim. There was no specific naval uniform, with levend sailors dressed like their land equivalents. The 31st Jannissary Orta wore blue coats. Officers could be distinguished by gold embroidery and elaborate weaponry.

The Ottomans could call upon irregular naval forces, particularly the Barbary Corsairs. The British allied with them to use ports and even ship repair facilities, while other western states, including Denmark and the United States, fought wars against them. The Barbary States had conventional frigates, brigs and sloops as well as xebecs and galleys. For example, Algeria had five smaller frigates, three xebecs and seven galleys. In addition, Algiers harbour was heavily fortified with over one hundred cannons.

An Ottoman squadron did enter the Adriatic with the Russian fleet under Ushakov. Still, otherwise, it was mainly smaller ships that could be seen operating from the Greek ports and the small Bosnian Dalmatian enclave of Neum. The main fleet actions were against the Russian and British fleets at Istanbul and Mount Athos.

Montenegro

The Montenegrins were recognised as excellent light infantry armed with a musket, pistols, sword, dagger and cartridge pouch. Constant practice since childhood made them sharpshooters. They had no concept of prisoners of war, cutting the heads off their enemies unless they surrendered before the battle. These heads could be hung from their necks or behind the shoulder, which added to the effect on morale when attacking! Ambushes, feigned retreats and night attacks were popular stratagems; otherwise, they made good use of cover, preferably from higher ground. However, discipline was poor, such as attacking when the enemy was sighted and looting at every opportunity. They could return to their homes with loot, making a long campaign challenging. The wives of fighters could accompany them on campaigns, carrying provisions and defending them with pistols and daggers if required. Montenegrin men were noted for their above-average height. They wore a white cloth coat called a *belača* and a shirt that reached down to the knee. A shawl (*struka*) was used instead of a blanket, and a red cap with a black tassel was worn.

Montenegrin fighter (Voyage historique et politique au Montenegro)

The inhabitants of the Bay of Cattaro, the Bokez, dressed differently from the other Illyrian Slavs. They typically wore baggy Greek trousers that reached mid-calf and jackets with silver buttons, lined with braid and lace and decorated with copper and silver plates. In addition, they wore a distinctive round hat over a velvet cap, red for Orthodox and black for Catholics. Half-boots were worn at home and sandals for travelling. Weapons included a triangular dagger (*khanjar*), a sword (*yataghan*), a pair of pistols and a long musket. Weapons were often highly decorated with carvings and inset stones or mother of pearl.

Company organisation was based on villages, brought together as a corps under the command of a *serdar*. Each company elected their leader after a *husting* in which candidates recounted their exploits and showed their wounds. The elected chief then took an oath with the flag in hand, and the whole company drew their swords and shouted, 'For the cross, for the faith, for the Holy Mother of God, for the White Tsar and the Fatherland, we swear by the bones of our ancestors, by their glory, to serve to the last drop of blood and never beg for or give any mercy, to die or be victorious!'

Long after the original Russian efforts in the Adriatic, they supported the Montenegrins, financially and militarily. Admiral Freemantle reported in 1812 that 'the Montenegrins have a Russian general, three colonels and many other officers with them.'[22]

Austria

Austria was a consistent partner in the various coalitions against Napoleon, although they were also at loggerheads with the Russians and Prussians. They held valuable provinces in Italy at the outset of the Napoleonic Wars and extensive territory along the Dalmatian coast. However, the Austrians territorial losses in the Adriatic were usually a consequence of defeats in central Europe. The Austrian army suffered from poor leadership, with Archduke Charles being the best of a poor bunch. The economy was weak, which meant the peacetime army was small, and mobilisation took time, not helped by the autonomy enjoyed by the Hungarians. Finally, their strategy, particularly the cordon system and linear tactics, were outdated, and there was considerable resistance to reform, from the Emperor and the bureaucratic elites.

The main Austrian units in Croatia were the Grenz regiments, which we first met in chapter three, and outside the Military Border, Croats contributed to line regiments. A reserve battalion was held on the borders when the field battalions joined the main armies. The Grenz regiments had around three thousand men each. They were organised differently from Austrian line regiments, with no grenadiers and an attachment of Serezaners for courier and scouting duties. There were seventeen regiments in total, with eight regiments in Croatia and three in Slavonia. Grenz Hussar units were more prevalent on the Hungarian border, but companies were raised mostly in wartime. In 1795, Grenzer cavalry were detached for fear of being infected by disaffection among the regiments. The four Hussar squadrons were formed into a provisional Banatisch-Slavonisch-Croatisch Granz Husaren Corps[23]. This unit appears to have been renumbered as Hussar Regiment No. 12, disbanded in 1801, and replaced by the Palatinal Regiment in 1802[24]. Grenz infantry wore a brown jacket and blue breeches from 1808, although some units may have retained the white service dress. It was not unusual in this period for commanders to ascribe racial stereotypes. Serbs and Croats were described as 'doughty fighters [who] consumed vast quantities of strong liquors'![25]

In June 1808, the Austrians created second-line forces called the Landwehr, which received twenty-one days of training a year and could be called up during wartime to engage in guerrilla activities and garrison fortresses. The more able and willing members formed *freicorps* (volunteer) units. The Dalmatian Freicorps was a battalion-strength unit formed from retired grenzers, wearing Dalmatian civilian dress, that was commanded by Major Dominik Ertel. It was disbanded in 1801. Others raised in the Turkish war (1788-89) served in Italy, including Gyulai's Croatian Corps of twelve companies and three hussar squadrons. They wore a brown jacket with red facings and blue Hungarian breeches. By the 1813 campaign, Landwehr battalions had been incorporated within the line infantry regiments.

The Grenz reserve battalions could not hold back Marmont's attack in 1809, not helped by a French-inspired Bosnian attack across the border. He advanced through the border to join Napoleon in Vienna. The Austrian commander Baron Knežević did manage to rally the Grenzer, repulse the Ottomans, and then move into Dalmatia, capturing Zadar. In 1813, the Austrian invasion of the French Illyrian Provinces included four battalions of Grenzer, two of line infantry, and six squadrons of the 5th Hussars. As the Grenzer regiments in French service mutinied, they were rearmed and reincorporated into the Austrian army.

CHAPTER SEVEN

CONCLUSION

The Congress of Vienna decided that Austria should regain the Illyrian provinces and take Ragusa, Lombardy and Venetia. The Grand Duchies of Tuscany and Modena were reinstated with Habsburg princes, and the Papal States were restored to the Pope. Piedmont, Nice and Savoy with the former Republic of Genoa were returned to the King of Sardinia. Ferdinand was reinstated as King of Naples and Sicily. The British held onto the Ionian Islands until ceding them to Greece in 1864.

This largely returned the region to the pre-war status quo without resolving pre-war issues. However, the genie of Italian unification was out of the bottle, and was achieved after much more bloodshed in 1861. In the Balkans, the Ottoman Empire continued to decline, with the individual states achieving independence after further Russo-Turkish wars and the collapse of the Austro-Hungarian Empire in 1918. Ali Pasha eventually pushed his luck with the Porte too far, starting a rebellion when he was ordered to resign from his position. In March 1821, an Ottoman army led by Hurshid Pasha cornered him in Ioannina. He was tricked into leaving the castle and died in a shoot-out with the official sent to execute him. Ali's rebellion helped the early stages of the Greek War of Independence, which was declared in the Peloponnese on 21 February 1821. In Croatia and Slovenia, Napoleon's Illyrian Provinces, with their legal code and administration, gave the people an insight into a different form of government, even if the burden of taxation meant they welcomed the return of the Austrians. They were also allowed to use their languages, with South Slavic 'Illyrian' becoming an official language. This led to the Illyrian Movement based in Zagreb, which played a role in the events that led to the revolutions of 1848.

The Adriatic was never a major theatre of operations during the Napoleonic Wars. However, it was part of the overall strategy of most of the combatants. It had an important role in the conflict, influencing alliances and diverting troops and ships, which all contributed to the defeat of Napoleon. Like most wars, the Napoleonic Wars caused personal and economic misery for most of the region's inhabitants.

Today, the main invaders are the thousands of tourists who descend on the Adriatic coast each summer, attracted by the sun, sea, food and fantastic scenery. In places, the heritage of the Napoleonic Wars can be seen. The fortresses at Pula, Senj, Klis, Vis, Dubrovnik, Kotor, Corfu and others are a tangible reminder of the strategic positions that the combatants held. The museums are typically small but well worth a visit, particularly the maritime museums at Pula, Kotor, and Vis. It's also worth going a little off the usual tourist routes to visit the lands of Ali Pasha in Albania and Epirus in northern Greece. He is remembered, though not always kindly as at Souli, in his birthplace at Tepelenë, his forts at Butrint and Palermos, and most importantly at Ioannina. So, as you enjoy your holiday, take a moment to remember those who fought and died in the Adriatic region.

APPENDIX 1

Chronology

April 1796: Napoleon Bonaparte takes command of the French army in Italy.
June 1796: General Aubert du Bayet arrives with French military mission in Constantinople.
August 1796: Treaty of San Ildefonso between France and Spain forces the British to evacuate the Mediterranean in the face of the combined French and Spanish fleets.
January 1797: Battle of Rivoli. Austrian defeat by Napoleon clears the Austrians from Italy and opens the way for an invasion of Austria.
April 1797: Peace of Loeben. With the French nearing Vienna, the Austrians sue for an armistice.
June 1797: French occupation of the Ionian Islands under the Venetian flag
October 1797: Treaty of Campo Formio. The Republic of Venice is disbanded, and its territories are divided between Austria and France. The Ionian Islands go to France.
November 1797: The Ionian Islands are annexed to France.
July 1798: Napoleon lands in Egypt.
September 1798: Alliance between Russia and the Ottoman Empire against France (official treaty January 1799).
October 1798: Ali Pasha captures mainland French enclaves at Butrint and Preveza.
December 1798: British/Russian/Ottoman Alliance.

March 1799: Russo-Ottoman forces capture Corfu ending French rule of the Ionian Islands. Septinsular Republic is created under Ottoman sovereignty in March 1800, then later becomes a Russian protectorate.

June 1799: Austria joins the Second Coalition.

November 1799: Napoleon becomes First Consul of France.

June 1800: Battle of Marengo destroys the Austrian army in Italy, leading to the end of the Second Coalition in February 1801.

March 1801: Tsar Paul is assassinated. Alexander comes to the throne.

March 1802: Peace of Amiens.

June 1802: Treaty of Paris. France and the Ottoman Empire restore relations.

February 1804: First Serbian Uprising.

December 1804: Napoleon crowned Emperor of the French.

April 1805: War of the Third Coalition. It ends with the Austrian surrender at Austerlitz (Dec. 1805), although Russia and Britain remain at war with France.

September 1805: Russo-Turkish defensive treaty.

December 1805: Treaty of Pressburg. Venetia, Istria and Dalmatia (down to Cattaro) are incorporated into the Kingdom of Italy with Napoleon as king.

January 1806: Russian fleet (Admiral Senyavin) arrives in Corfu and, with Montenegro, contests the Adriatic with the French. Occupies the Bay of Cattaro.

May 1806: France occupies the Republic of Ragusa (Dubrovnik) and defeats a Russian and Montenegrin siege.

October 1806: Battle of Castelnuovo. Russian and Montenegrin troops defeat the French.

October 1806: War of the Fourth Coalition. Prussia and Russia are defeated.

December 1806: Russo-Turkish War starts. Ends with the Treaty of Bucharest (May 1812).

February 1807: Anglo-Turkish War starts with a British squadron defeating an Ottoman naval force in the Sea of Marmora, threatening Istanbul.

May 1807: Sultan Selim III deposed. Mustafa IV accedes to the Ottoman throne.

July 1807: Battle of Athos. Russians destroy the Turkish fleet.

July 1807: Treaty of Tilsit. Russia returns the Ionian Islands to France.

July 1808: Sultan Mustafa IV deposed; accession of Mahmud II.

January 1809: Treaty of the Dardanelles—Britain and Ottoman peace treaty.

April 1809: Austria returns to the conflict with the War of the Fifth Coalition. It ends in defeat at Wagram in July 1809.

October 1809: Treaty of Schonbrunn. Austria loses what remained of its Adriatic coast, Carinthia, and the Croat and Banal districts of the Austrian Military Border.

October 1809: Napoleon creates the Illyrian Provinces, incorporating all the former Venetian and Austrian territory in the Balkans.

October 1809: British forces capture the Ionian Islands of Zakynthos, Cephalonia, Ithaca, and Kythira, followed by Lefkada in April 1810. Corfu, Parga, and Paxos are left under French control.

October 1810: Failed French attempt to capture Lissa (Vis).

March 1811: Naval Battle of Lissa. British defeat the French invasion force.

April 1812: British garrison and fortify Lissa.

May 1812: Treaty of Bucharest. Russia gains Bessarabia and Serbs achieve limited autonomy.

June 1812: Napoleon invades Russia. Sixth Coalition formed.

June 1813: Ragusan revolt is supported by the British fleet and Austrian troops. French capitulate in January 1814.

August 1813: Austria joins the War of the Sixth Coalition after Napoleon retreats from Moscow and invades the Illyrian Provinces.

December 1813: Zara (Zadar) surrenders after Austrian siege.

January 1814: Montenegrins capture the Bay of Cattaro with British help.

January 1814: Ragusa surrenders to British and Austrian troops, who put down attempts to return the Republic's independence.

April/May 1814: Napoleon abdicates, and the Treaty of Paris returns France to 1792 boundaries. Austria reoccupies the Illyrian Provinces, including the Bay of Cattaro and Ragusa.

April 1815: Second Serbian Uprising.

May 1815: Austrians defeat Murat at Tolentino, ending his rule of the Kingdom of Naples.

APPENDIX 2

Wargaming the Adriatic Conflicts

Introduction to wargaming

Wargamers use model soldiers to simulate battles, real or fictional. The game developed out of chess and the military war games used by the Prussian general staff in the 19th century. The modern hobby started in the 1950s, and despite computer and board games, it is still a thriving hobby today with monthly magazines and clubs worldwide. It is most popular in the English-speaking world, with a focus on the UK and USA. Players can play solo, with friends, or in a club setting.

Unlike chess, there are hundreds of different rule sets, each covering a specific historical period, although around fifty or so are played in significant numbers. They usually start with a points system for each army to create a balanced game, and rules for setting out the battlefield terrain. Once the troops are on the table, the rules set out how fast each unit can move, followed by rules for shooting and then hand-to-hand combat. Records are kept for casualties, or figures are removed from the table. Finally, rules determine the morale of each unit and the army as a whole. Dice or cards of various types are used to determine the chance element.

The figures are generally made of metal or plastic and are hand-painted. In a historical game, this involves researching the army's uniforms, organisation and tactics. The models come in various sizes, from 2mm to 54mm high, and are made by figure manufacturers worldwide. Most wargamers have many different armies that they collect on a project basis. For a detailed introduction to this fascinating hobby, the reader can do no better than consulting *The Wargaming Compendium* by Henry Hyde (Pen & Sword, 2013).

The Napoleonic period is one of the most popular with wargamers. In the latest Great Wargaming Survey (WSS, 2021), the Napoleonic period came second behind the Second World War. Wargamers are attracted to the period for many reasons, including the colourful uniforms, the availability of sources, film coverage, the wide range of combatant nations, and the combination of infantry, cavalry and artillery. This popularity led to many different rulesets and models for just about every army that fought in the Napoleonic Wars. As Henry Hyde put it, 'The Napoleonic Wars have a magical appeal—the games look glorious, whether large or small, and set in the desolate wintry wastelands of Russia or the sweltering heat of the Spanish plains. The balance between the three arms of infantry, cavalry and artillery is nearly perfect, with none completely dominating the other, and tactical success demands a keen eye for ground and tremendous timing.'

Wargame rules

There are dozens of rulesets for the Napoleonic period, which is pretty daunting for the beginner, so we will focus on the most widely played systems. If we travel back to 1977, when Bruce Quarrie published his first edition of *Napoleon's Campaigns in Miniature* (Patrick Stephens Limited), rules were typically pretty complicated. Bruce's playing rules included national characteristics for the main nations and their units, and detailed charts for moving, firing, melee and morale. His campaign rules even had the cost of recruiting and supplying each soldier in pounds and shillings! Thankfully, modern rulesets are much simpler, with many of these factors abstracted to speed up play. They also recognise that modern houses are typically smaller. So games have to be played on a table no bigger than six or eight feet by four feet or smaller. Current rules are usually flexible enough to accommodate different basing conventions (the number of figures on one base) and different figure scales.

Napoleonic battles could be massive, and the biggest battles are difficult to reproduce on the tabletop. Although these were rare in the Balkans (other than the Russo-Ottoman War), the solution is to scale up each unit on the tabletop. A good example is *Blucher* by Sam Mustafa, where each unit represents 2,000-3,000 infantry in 4-6 battalions, less for cavalry. This means you can command a corps, or even an army, making grand tactical decisions rather than the detail of unit combat.

For mid-sized battles, a tabletop unit typically represents a battalion of 500-1,000 infantry. These rules will cover the larger actions in the Adriatic, such as the Russian 1806 campaign, the French response, and the armies of Ali Pasha. Sam Mustafa has written *Lasalle* for games at this level, where you might typically command a division. These illustrate the relative simplicity of modern rules with an emphasis on playability. After a few games, an experienced wargamer can rely on the Quick Reference Sheet (QRF) alone. For a similar or slightly larger scale (battalion or regiment), Hervé Caille has written *Bataille Empire*, an adaptation of his popular ancient rules *L'Art de la Guerre* (ADLG). These are a little more complex, but if you have played the ancient rules, you will be familiar with the basic mechanisms. According to at least one survey, the most popular Napoleonic wargames set of rules is the battalion-sized game *Black Powder* (Warlord Games) written by Rick Priestley and Jervis Johnson. These are unashamedly abstracted rules with plenty of fun elements that don't take themselves too seriously.

As we have highlighted in this book's narrative, the Adriatic conflict was typically about the small war. For this, we need small battle or skirmish rules. While these are usually played with the larger 28mm figures, they can be played at the smaller figure scale on the dining table. At this scale, the cross-border raids along the Military Border and the island-hopping campaigns can be played with small forces of 40-80 figures on each side representing companies or even smaller units. *Sharp Practice* by Richard Clark (Too Fat Lardies) is a popular ruleset for large skirmishes, focusing on building characters and a narrative for your games. As the author puts it, 'It is better to die bravely than a coward, but sometimes dying humorously can be better still.' These rules emphasise command and control rather than the minutiae of weaponry. *Osprey Wargames* produce several good value rulesets at this scale. While written for North America, Dan Mersey's *Rebels and Patriots* works very well for our purposes. The mix of regular and irregular forces is similar to our region, and the game mechanics are straightforward, allowing new players to pick up the basics in a couple of moves. Mark Latham's *Chosen Men* is a similar system designed for the Napoleonic Wars, although a little more complex. If you have only collected a handful of figures, then *Fistful of Lead* (Wiley Games) is an excellent introductory skirmish game typically played with six to eight figures on each side. These fast and furious, card-activated rules are an excellent way engage your kids in the hobby.

We need to cover the all-important naval actions in the Adriatic. Naval wargaming can be complex, with rules covering the minutia of manoeuvring a sailing ship across the table. Wargamers on land do not have to worry about wind, currents and rocks, with troops that generally move as ordered. Gabrio Tolentino has successfully abstracted these complications in *Black Seas* (Warlord Games). The supplement to these rules, *Hold Fast!*, covers the more minor battles involving frigates, brigs and sloops that were common in the Adriatic. They also include lists for the Russians and Ottomans, often ignored in the fleet battle rules. There are more detailed rules, but these are a good starting point.

Ottoman and Russian ships clash in a game of *Black Seas*.

The above guide covers battles on the tabletop. However, we should not forget wargame campaigns. These can be as complex as you want or simply a mechanism for linking your tabletop battles. Many of the rules above have simple campaign systems. However, if you're going to tackle this subject in detail, then Henry Hyde's *Wargaming Campaigns* (Pen & Sword, 2022) shows you how. After an introduction to campaigns, there is a chapter on generalship and strategy, followed by how to write your own campaign rules. Most chapters give you the theory, followed by practical examples and his suggested rules to get you started. The book is well illustrated throughout, with instructive screen grabs. This book also includes a handy chapter on naval campaigns. There are reviews of all the rules mentioned above on the author's blog (https://balkandave.blogspot.com). A quick and often cheap way of downloading wargame rules is to visit the vast collection at Wargame Vault.

Wargame figures

If you have got this far, you will be looking for some wargame figures to manoeuvre around the tabletop. If money is no object, then there are second-hand figures to be purchased on eBay, and plenty of professional figure painters will turn your metal or plastic figures into the finished product. However, for most wargamers, this involves purchasing and painting the figures. Uniform colours are generally available on the internet or in the books listed in the bibliography. There are plenty of how-to guides to painting on YouTube and elsewhere that take the beginner through the basics. With modern paints and washes, very presentable results can be achieved without needing an art degree. It is also a very therapeutic aspect of the hobby, the perfect way to wind down after a busy day. The best advice is to purchase a small number of figures to get started, and build your collection as time and cash allow.

For those of a certain age, the early years of the hobby involved getting catalogues from a few manufacturers, or using the ubiquitous boxes of 1/72nd figures in the Airfix range. Today the wargamer has a vast array of ranges to choose from in every figure scale, covering just about every Napoleonic troop type and ships as well. A quick Google search for 'Napoleonic wargame figures' brings over six hundred thousand results!

Croatian Hussars. 28mm figures from Wargames Foundry

The first decision is the figure scale. If you want to fight the larger battles in our region, the smaller scales are the best choice. There are 6mm ranges from Baccus, Heroic and Ross, or the slightly larger 8mm figures from the Adler range. Do not worry about painting too much detail at this scale; you will be looking at the models from a couple of feet away, not through a magnifying glass. Slightly larger with more detail are the 10mm ranges from Pendraken, Old Glory and others. For the divisional games, 15mm is a good option. AB Miniatures are lovely sculpts at this scale, although quite large and expensive. Essex and Old Glory have comprehensive good-quality ranges. For the smaller battles and skirmish games, 28mm figures are ideal. There are extensive ranges by the bigger firms, including Front Rank, Foundry, Perry, Warlord, Old Glory and Essex, and many smaller firms. While metal figures are not cheap, plastic figures are increasingly popular at this scale. Vitrix, Perry and Warlord produce boxes of good-value, finely-sculpted models with a range of options. However, these require some assembly, which is pretty straightforward but takes more preparation time. There are also a large number of companies producing plastic figures in 1/72nd scale (20mm), although these are mostly made from softer plastic. Some wargamers play skirmish games with 40mm or 54mm figures, and Vitrix does plastic figures at this scale, although the troop types are limited. For ships, Warlord makes all you will need in their Black Seas range. For finer-detail models, Langton Miniatures does a comprehensive range in 1:1,200 scale, although these require some modelling skills.

The Madaxeman.com blog is a good resource for supplier directories and the Plastic Soldier Review for 1/72nd plastics.

You will also need a mat for your table. A simple light green or sandy cloth will do, and blue for naval battles, although there are some better options from Deep Cut, Cigar Box Battles and Tiny Wargames. Other gamers use polystyrene or MDF baseboards that can be bought or carved into realistic terrain surfaces. The terrain is best placed on top of the mat, and for our region, you will need plenty of hills, rivers and a few trees. Mediterranean-style buildings work for the Adriatic coast with its Venetian influences, and are available from several firms. Most terrain features can be modelled from scratch with basic modelling skills, and there are plenty of online resources. These are also comprehensively covered in *The Wargaming Compendium*.

For most of the standard troop and ship types, the ranges above will cover the main combatants in the Adriatic. However, there are a few challenges. Russian wargame figures typically have the post-1809 or 1812 shakos. Brigade Games in the USA has the former 28mm Vitrix range, but this can be an expensive option for European gamers. Several Ottoman ranges include Albanians and other troop types in the region, and irregular troops for the Greek War of Independence work as well. Steve Barber has a good 28mm range, which can be bulked out by Old Glory figures. Old Man's Creations does some lovely personality figures in resin, including Ali Pasha. Montenegrin troops are similar to the Greeks and Albanians but may need a little conversion work.

Ali Pasha and his Skipetars. 28mm figures from Old Man's Creations, Steve Barber Models, and Old Glory.

Scenarios

Wargame scenarios are a good way of getting started on wargaming typical actions of the period. We have included a couple of introductory scenarios here. However, more will be available on the author's website (www.balkan-history.org).

Battle of Bergatto Heights (Ragusa), June 1806.

Background

On 27 May 1806, French General Lauriston occupied the city of Ragusa (Dubrovnik) with a force of some three thousand men. The Russians and their Montenegrin and Bokez allies responded by seizing the port of Old Ragusa (Cavtat) on 3 June, forcing the French outposts back to the Bergatto Heights, a strong defensive position to the east of Ragusa. The Russian fleet and Bokez gunboats arrived off Ragusa on 13 June to blockade the city, which forced French reinforcements to travel the longer inland route. The French built three artillery strongpoints on the Bergatto Heights, supported by French infantry and some Ragusan militia. The Russian commander Admiral Senyavin ordered his forces to attack the heights. The classification is for *Black Powder*, but these can easily be adapted for other rules.

Opposing Forces

Russian sources claim three thousand French infantry and four thousand Ragusan militia defended the heights. This has to be an exaggeration, as it would have left the city without a French garrison. While the Ragusans marginally favoured the French over the Russians, it is unlikely that so many would have been mobilised to fight for the French in such a short time. Lauriston would also have been wary of relying on them. The Russians had twelve hundred regular troops and thirty-five hundred Montenegrin and Bokez fighters. There would be some naval gunfire support to shell the French right flank.

French: General Lauriston

Two battalions of French line infantry: Standard, Musket, Pas de Charge, Reliable.
One battalion of French light infantry: Standard, Musket, Pas de Charge, Skirmish.
Three medium gun batteries.
One battalion of Ragusan militia: Standard, Irregular, Musket, Freshly-raised.
The French would be behind improvised rock defences on a steep hill. Classify as soft cover because they were probably not high or substantial enough to qualify as hard cover.

Russian: Prince Vyazemskiy

One battalion Vitebsk Musketeers: Standard, Musket, Steady.
One battalion 13th Jagers: Standard, Musket, Steady, Skirmish.
Four units of Montenegrin/Bokez irregulars: Standard, Musket, Irregular, Bloodthirsty, Unreliable.
One heavy battery, representing shipboard guns. The French position was on a steep cliff, making it difficult to elevate enough guns.

Objective

The Russians have to capture two of the gun positions, after which the French will withdraw.

Russian 13th Jagers on the left pin the French, while the Montenegrins attack the gun battery.

Historical battle

The Russians organised a hasty attack after being warned by the Ottomans that French reinforcements were en route. The Montenegrins attacked the French left flank by scaling the heights. After a forward position was captured by the Montenegrins, they impulsively moved towards the next position. Four companies of the 13th Jagers, under Captain Babichev, scaled the heights to support them. As the French prepared a counterattack, Prince Vyazemskiy attacked with his remaining forces in four columns. These troops gained the top of the heights, reorganised, and attacked the main French position. The French withdrew to the heights above Ragusa and then into the city. Both sides lost around four hundred men, and some French prisoners were decapitated by the Montenegrin fighters.

The Russians followed up this victory with an unsuccessful assault on the island of San Marco opposite the city harbour. They then tightened the siege, mounting naval guns on the heights above the city. General Molitor arrived with French reinforcements on 6 July, turning the Montenegrin position. This move threatened the Russian rear, and the Montenegrins dispersed with their plunder from the villas outside the city. Senyavin, therefore, ordered his troops to embark and return to Cattaro (Kotor).

Grado, 29 June 1810

Background

Captain William Hoste had returned to the Adriatic in 1810, commanding a squadron that included the frigates *Amphion*, *Active* and *Cerberus*, and the sloop *Acorn*. They were so successful that prizes became scarce, so he and his captains made bold efforts to cut out ships from fortified harbours. One such attack was on the port of Grado, near Trieste. Hoste had heard that a convoy carrying naval supplies to Venice was sheltering under the protection of two ruined forts with a garrison of only twenty-five French troops. He assembled all the ships' boats, although *Active*'s were delayed. They landed and marched towards the town, covered by carronades in the ships' boats. However, the estimate of the garrison proved inaccurate, as a strong force of French troops and local militia debouched from the town and attacked the landing parties. The British marines and sailors fought off this attack and, supported by the arriving boats from *Active*, captured the town. As they were cutting out the convoy, the French launched a counterattack which was also beaten off. Five prizes and fifteen smaller craft were sailed to Lissa, and eleven larger ships were burnt.

Opposing forces

This is a small battle best played with skirmish rules. The classification here is for *Rebels & Patriots* with upgrades in brackets. The seaman units are six model skirmish units, while the rest are standard twelve-figure units. For the first six turns firing ranges are reduced to twelve inches due to darkness.

French

One unit of French line infantry at the landing beach.
One unit of French line infantry in the town.
Two units of Italian line infantry (Green) in the town.
One unit of National Guard (Green, Timid, Poor Shooters).
For the counterattack—Two units of French line infantry.

British

One unit of Marines (Light infantry, Veteran, Good Shooters).
Three units of Seamen (Skirmishers, Veteran, Aggressive).
Two boat-mounted medium artillery.
Arriving in the town later: two units of Seamen (Skirmishers, Veteran, Aggressive).

Objective

The British must hold the town for six moves in order to cut out the prizes.

A British landing party attacks a farm defended
by the French Royal Dalmatian Legion.

What-if?

Historians typically dislike counterfactual history or the 'what-if'. Counterfactual history explores history and historical incidents by extrapolating a timeline in which key historical events either did not occur or had an outcome different from the actual historical result. The critics argue that while it is entertaining, it does not meet the standards of mainstream historical research due to its speculative nature. Wargamers have no such inhibitions, and often play games that involve armies that never actually fought or campaigns that might have but did not happen.

The Napoleonic Wars in the Balkans have many such options. For example, as we have seen, the Russians offered to march across the Balkans to attack the French on the Adriatic. The British only declined the offer because they would have to supply the troops. Napoleon could have used the Ionian Islands as a jumping-off point for a full-scale invasion of the Ottoman Empire, possibly in conjunction with the Austrians or the Russians at different times. This is not simply fantasy, because Napoleon indicated this vision in a message to the Directory after the Italian campaign. These scenarios and many others provide entertaining alternatives to traditional games.

BIBLIOGRAPHY

Admiralty, Lords Commissioners, *The Adriatic Pilot* (Hydrographic Office, 1861, HardPress Kindle edition, 2017)

Anderson, R., *Naval Wars in the Levant* (Liverpool University Press, 1952)

Anon. *Service Afloat or The Naval Career of Sir William Hoste* (W. H. Allen, 1887)

Anon. *Uniforms of the Royal Sussex Regiment* (The Royal Sussex Regiment Museum Trust, 1989)

Anscombe, F., *The Ottoman Balkans, 1750-1830* (Wiener, 2005)

Askan, V., *Ottoman Wars 1700-1870* (Pearson, 2007)

Baggally, J., *Ali Pasha and Great Britain* (Blackwell, 1938)

Bartov, O., and Weitz, E., *Shatterzone of Empires: Coexistence and Violence in the German, Habsburg, Russian, and Ottoman Borderlands* (Indiana University Press, 2013)

Black, J., *European Warfare 1660-1815* (UCL Press, 1998)

Boggis-Rolfe, C., *Adriatic: A Two-Thousand-Year History of the Sea, Lands and Peoples* (Amberley, 2022)

Brnardic, V., *Napoleon's Balkan Troops* (Osprey, 2004)

Broers, M., *The Napoleonic Mediterranean* (I. B. Tauris, 2021)

Bronevskiy, V., *Northern Tars in Southern Waters* (Helion, 2019)

Brummett, P., *The Fortress: Defining and Mapping the Ottoman Frontier* (Proceedings of the British Academy 156, 2009)

Calic, M., *The Great Cauldron* (Harvard University Press, 2019)

Carter, T., *Historical Record of the Forty-Fourth or the East Essex Regiment* (Gale and Polden, 1887)

Chandler, D., *The Campaigns of Napoleon* (Weidenfeld & Nicolson, 1966)
Chartrand, R., *Émigré and Foreign Troops in British Service (1) 1793-1802* (Osprey, 1999)
Chartrand, R., *Émigré and Foreign Troops in British Service (2) 1803-1815* (Osprey, 2000)
Chartrand, R., *Napoleon's Sea Soldiers* (Osprey, 1990)
Christophe, R., *Le Maréchal Marmont, Duc de Raguse* (Hachette, 1968)
Christopher of Perrevo and Chiliarchos, *History of Suli and Parga* (Constable, 1823)
Crowdy, T., *French Warship Crews* (Osprey, 2005)
Dempsey, G., *Napoleon's Mercenaries* (Greenhill Books, 2016)
Ede-Borrett, S., *The Army of the Kingdom of Italy 1805-1814* (Helion, 2022)
Elting, J., *Swords Around a Throne: Napoleon's Grande Armée* (The Free Press, 1989)
Feather, M., *HMS Amphion 1798* (Feather, 2015)
Flaherty, C., *The Napoleonic Ottoman Army* (Partizan Press, 2019)
Fleming, K., *The Muslim Bonaparte* (Princeton Legacy Library, 1999)
Fregosi, P., *Dreams of Empire* (Hutchinson, 1989)
Frumin, M and Saul, K., *Reading Between the Lines: Admiral Ushakov's Relations with Kapudane Abdülkadir Beg According to Russian and Ottoman Sources* (International Symposium on Piri Reis and Turkish Maritime History, September 2013,vol.4)
Glenny, M., *The Balkans 1804-1999* (Granta, 1999)
Glover, G., *The Forgotten War Against Napoleon: Conflict in the Mediterranean* (Pen & Sword, 2017)
Glover, G., *Fighting Napoleon: The Recollections of Lieutenant John Hildebrand 35th Foot* (Frontline, 2016)
Gosu, A., *The Third Anti-Napoleonic Coalition and the Sublime Porte* (International Journal of Turkish Studies 9 No.1/2)
Gradeva, R., *Between Hinterland and Frontier: Ottoman Vidin, Fifteenth to Eighteenth Centuries* (Proceedings of the British Academy 156, 2009)
Grant, C., *Napoleon's Campaign in Egypt, Vol. 2* (Partizan Press, 2007)
Hajdarpasic, E., *Frontier Anxieties* (Austrian History Yearbook, Volume 51, May 2020)
Halpern, J. and B., *A Serbian Village in Historical Perspective* (Irvington, 1984)
Hardy, M., *The British and Vis: War in the Adriatic 1805-15* (Archaeopress, 2009)
Hardy, M., *The British Navy, Rijeka and A. L. Adamic* (Archaeopress, 2005)

Harris, R., *Dubrovnik: A History* (Saqi, 2006)
Haythornthwaite, P., *Napoleon's Military Machine* (Spellmount, 1988)
Haythornthwaite, P., *Wellington's Military Machine* (Spellmount, 1989)
Haythornthwaite, P., *The Napoleonic Source Book* (Guild Publishing, 1990)
Haythornthwaite, P., *The Russian Army of the Napoleonic Wars (1): Infantry, 1799-1814* (Osprey, 1987)
Haythornthwaite, P., *Austrian Army of the Napoleonic Wars (1): Infantry* (Osprey, 1986)
Haythornthwaite, P., *Austrian Army of the Napoleonic Wars (2): Cavalry* (Osprey, 1986)
Henderson, J., *The Frigates: An Account of the Lighter Warships of the Napoleonic Wars* (Leo Cooper, 1994)
Hickok, M., *Ottoman Military Administration in Eighteenth-Century Bosnia* (Brill, 1997)
Hirst, A. and Salmon, P., *The Ionian Islands: Aspects of their History and Culture* (Cambridge, 2014)
Holland, H., *Travels in the Ionian Islands, Albania, Thessaly, Macedonia During the Years 1812 and 1813* (Longman, 1815)
Hollins, D., *Austrian Grenadiers and Infantry 1788-1816* (Osprey, 1998)
Hollins, D., *Austrian Frontier Troops 1740-98* (Osprey, 2005)
Hopton, R., *The Battle of Maida 1806* (Leo Cooper, 2002)
Irving, C., *The Adriatic Islands and Corfu* (Dent, 1971)
Ismail, F., *The Making of the Treaty of Bucharest, 1811-12* (Middle Eastern Studies Vol. 15, No. 2, May 1979)
Isom-Verhaaren, C., *The Sultan's Fleet* (I.B.Tauris, 2022)
Jelavich, B., *The History of the Balkans: Eighteenth and Nineteenth Centuries* (Cambridge, 1983)
Johnson, R., *Napoleonic Armies: A Wargamer's Campaign Directory 1805-1815* (Arms & Armour, 1984)
Johnson, R., *The Corsican—A Diary of Napoleon's Life in His Own Words* (Pickle Partners, 2011)
Johnson, W., *The Crescent Among the Eagles* (Private, 1994)
Kagan, F. and Higham, R., *The Military History of Tsarist Russia* (Palgrave, 2002)
Karpat, K. and Zens, R., *Ottoman Borderlands: Issues, Personalities, and Political Changes* (Wisconsin, 2004)

Knežević, S. and Vukićević, B., *Montenegrin-British Military Cooperation Against the French in the Bay of Kotor 1813-1814* (War in History. Volume 28: Number 4, 2021)

Laird, W., *The Royal Navy: a History from the Earliest Times to the Present Day* (Marston, 1897)

Lavery, B., *Nelson's Navy: Ships, Men, Organisation 1793-1815* (Conway, 1989)

Lieven, D., *The Cambridge History of Russia, Vol.II* (Cambridge, 2015)

Mackesy, P., *The War in the Mediterranean 1803-1810* (Longmans, 1957)

Malcolm, N., *Rebels, Believers, Survivors: Studies in the History of the Albanians* (Oxford, 2020)

Malcolm, N., *Bosnia: A Short History* (Macmillan, 1996)

Martin, R., *History of the British Possessions in the Mediterranean* (Whittaker, 1837)

May, W., *The Boats of Men of War* (Caxton, 2003)

McNeill, W., *Europe's Steppe Frontier* (Chicago, 1964)

Mikaberidze, A., *Kutuzov: A Life in War and Peace* (Oxford, 2022)

Mikhailovsky-Danilevsky, A., *Russo-Turkish War of 1806-1812* (Nafziger Collection, 2002)

Nichols, A., *Wellington's Mongrel Regiment* (Spellmount, 2005)

Norwich, J., *Venice, The Greatness and the Fall* (Allen Lane, 1981)

Oman, C., *My Adventures During the Late War* (Edward Arnold, 1902)

Örenç, A., *Albanian Soldiers in the Ottoman Army During the Greek Revolt at 1821* (2nd İnternational Balkan Annual Conference [IBAC] 2012, c. 2, Tirana 2013, pp. 352-524)

Ozguven, B., *Palanka Forts and Construction Activity in the Late Ottoman Balkans* (Proceedings of the British Academy, 156, 2009)

Pivka, O., *Napoleon's Italian and Neapolitan Troops* (Osprey, 1979)

Planert, U., *Napoleon's Empire* (Palgrave, 2016)

Plomer, W., *The Diamond of Jannina* (Jonathan Cape, 1970)

Pocock, T., *Remember Nelson: The Life of Captain Sir William Hoste* (Lume Books Kindle edition, 2020)

Pocock, T., *Stopping Napoleon: War and Intrigue in the Mediterranean* (John Murray, 2004)

Potts, J., *The Ionian Islands and Epirus* (Signal Books, 2010)

Pouqueville, F., *Travels in Epirus, Albania, Macedonia and Thessaly* (London, 1820)

Price, A., *The Eyes of the Fleet* (Grafton, 1992)

Quarrie, B., *Napoleon's Campaigns in Miniature* (Patrick Stephens, 1986)
Rothenberg, G., *Napoleon's Great Adversary* (Spellmount, 1982)
Rothenberg, G., *The Military Border in Croatia, 1740-1881* (Chicago, 1966)
Russell, Q. and A., *Ali Pasha, Lion of Ioannina* (Pen & Sword, 2017)
Sakul, K., *Ottoman Attempts to Control the Adriatic Frontier in the Napoleonic Wars* (Proceedings of the British Academy, 156, 2009)
Sapherson, C., and Lenton, J., *Navy Lists from the Age of Sail*, (Raider Games, 1985)
Saul, N., *Russia and the Mediterranean 1797-1807* (University of Chicago, 1970)
Shaw, S., *History of the Ottoman Empire and Modern Turkey*, Vol. 1 (Cambridge, 1976)
Smith, D., *Napoleon's Regiments* (Greenhill, 2000)
Stein, M., *Military Service and Material Gain on the Ottoman Hapsburg Frontier* (Proceedings of the British Academy, 156, 2009)
Sumrada, J., (Editor), *Napoleon na Jadranu* (Zaloba Annales, 2006)
Trimen, R., *An Historical Memoir of the 35th Royal Sussex Regiment of Foot* (Southampton, 1873)
Uyar, M., and Erickson, E., *A Military History of the Ottomans: From Osman to Ataturk* (Praeger, 2009)
Valentini, Major-General, *Military Reflections on Turkey* (Pallas Armata reprint, 1995)
White, F., *The Russian Navy in Trieste. During the Wars of the Revolution and the Empire* (The American Slavic and East European Review, Vol. 6, No. 3/4, Dec. 1947)
Wittman, W., *Travels in Turkey, Asia-Minor and Syria* (Phillips, 1803)
Woodman, R., *The Victory of Seapower* (Chatham, 1998)
Yener, E., *Ottoman Seapower and Naval Technology during Catherine II's Turkish Wars 1768-1792* (International Naval Journal, 2016, Vol. 9, Issue 1)
Zens, R., *Pasvanoglu Osman Pasha and the Pashalik of Belgrade 1791-1807* (International Journal of Turkish Studies, Vol. 8, No. 1, Spring 2002)

ACKNOWLEDGMENTS

I am grateful to the many writers and historians who inspired my interest in the history of the Balkans and who contributed to my understanding of the region. I am also indebted to the people of the Balkans, who have been so welcoming during my many visits, even when walking over their property to examine a long-forgotten battlefield or fortification. To these, I would add fellow enthusiasts who have contributed ideas and content through the website *Balkan Military History* (www.balkanhistory.org) during the twenty-three years I have been its editor.

First and foremost, I must thank my wife Liz for her support and tolerance of the countless hours I have spent writing, blogging, tweeting and gaming about the Balkans—not to mention the 'holidays'. I also thank her for proofreading many of my outputs, with the same patience she showed to her pupils during her years as an inspirational teacher. The same applies to our brilliant daughter Jessica, who I forgive for becoming a scientist rather than a historian, despite more trips to the Balkans than any other British teenager is likely to endure.

I would also thank the many wargaming friends who now have a greater understanding of Balkan history than any gamer ought to have. Even when playing games far removed from the Balkans, they look closely for a link, which is often there! These include the wargame suppliers who have produced model ranges for wars far from the mainstream of our hobby.

My thanks to all those institutions and their staff who assisted with the research for this book, including, but not limited to: The National Archives Kew, The British Library, The National Library of Scotland, and the many museums and contacts in the countries that make up the Balkans today who have been so generous with their time during my visits.

Finally, my thanks to Henry Hyde for the cover design and Author Help, including Sarah Woodfin for her editing. All errors are my own.

ENDNOTES

Prologue
1. C. Oman, *My Adventures During the Late War*, (Edward Arnold, 1902), p. 304.
2. V. Bronevskiy, *Northern Tars in Southern Waters*, (Helion, 2019), p. 98.
3. V. Bronevskiy, *Northern Tars in Southern Waters*, (Helion, 2019), p. 173.
4. G. Glover, *Fighting Napoleon*, (Frontline, 2016), p. 184.
5. Anon., *Service Afloat or The Naval Career of Sir William Hoste*, (W. H. Allen, 1887), p. 149.
6. These issues are discussed by P. Ballinger, in her chapter *Liquid Borderland, Inelastic Sea?: Mapping the Eastern Adriatic*, in Bartov, O. and Weitz, E., *Shatterzone of Empires: Coexistence and Violence in the German, Habsburg, Russian, and Ottoman Borderlands*, (Indiana University Press, 2013).
7. D. Gates, *The Napoleonic Wars 1803-1815*, (Pimlico, 2003).
8. Venice several times. The furthest down the east coast appears to have been Trieste on 30 April 1797.
9. On 11 March 1816. R. Johnson, *The Corsican—A Diary of Napoleon's Life in His Own Words*, (Pickle Partners, 2011), Location 6103.
10. C. Finkel, *Afterword: The Ottoman Frontier*, (Proceedings of the British Academy, 156, 2009), p. 540.
11. J. Black, *European Warfare 1660-1815*, (UCL Press, 1998), p. 172.
12. B. Quarrie, *Napoleon's Campaigns in Miniature*, (Patrick Stephens, 1986), p. 7.

Chapter 1
1. Treaty of Požarevac 1718.
2. Treaty of Belgrade 1739.
3. W. McNeill, *Europe's Steppe Frontier*, (Chicago, 1964), p. 202.
4. D. Lieven, *The Cambridge History of Russia, Vol.II*, (Cambridge, 2015), p. 514.
5. F. Kagan, *The Military History of Tsarist Russia*, (Palgrave, 2002), p. 125.
6. M. Calic, *The Great Cauldron*, (Harvard University Press, 2019), p. 181.

7. B. Mungai, *The Ottoman Army of the Napoleonic Wars 1789-1815*, (Helion, 2022), p. 168.
8. S. Shaw, *History of the Ottoman Empire and Modern Turkey, Vol 1*, (Cambridge, 1976), p. 260.
9. J. Norwich, *Venice, The Greatness and the Fall*, (Allen Lane, 1981), p. 355.
10. R. Anderson, *Naval Wars in the Levant*, (Liverpool University Press, 1952), p. 352.
11. Lords Commissioners Admiralty, *The Adriatic Pilot*, (Hydrographic Office, 1861), Location 368.
12. Luccio, V., *Treatise on the Currents in the Gulf of Venice* (Faden, 1806)
13. National Archives: HCA 45:58:27, Bolland of Trieste v Vincent (Captain of the sloop *Arrow*), March, 1804.

Chapter 2

1. Some historians argue that Napoleon made this up later to lend colour to his memoirs.
2. D. Chandler, *The Campaigns of Napoleon*, (Weidenfeld & Nicolson, 1966), p. 130.
3. 15 February 1797, R. Johnson, *The Corsican—A Diary of Napoleon's Life in His Own Words*, (Pickle Partners, 2011), Location 786.
4. R. Martin, *History of the British Possessions in the Mediterranean*, (Whittaker, 1837), p. 336.
5. J. Potts, *The Ionian Islands and Epirus*, (Signal Books, 2010), p. 42.
6. Plomer and the dates support Chabot as Gentili was not in post long, but Russell says Gentili.
7. Q. and A. Russell, *Ali Pasha, Lion of Ioannina*, (Pen & Sword, 2017), p. 70.
8. N. Saul, *Russia and the Mediterranean 1797-1807*, (University of Chicago, 1970), p. 80.
9. F. White, *The Russian Navy in Trieste. During the Wars of the Revolution and the Empire*, (The American Slavic and East European Review, Vol. 6, No. ¾, Dec., 1947), p. 27
10. Mitia Frumin and Kahraman Saul, *Reading Between the Lines: Admiral Ushakov's Relations with Kapudane Abdülkadir Beg According to Russian and Ottoman Sources*, (International Symposium on Piri Reis and Turkish Maritime History, September 2013, vol.4) pp.71-96.
11. National Archives: FO 42:3, Ionian Consul letters, January 1798 to December 1799.
12. P. Fregosi, *Dreams of Empire*, (Hutchinson, 1989), p. 141.
13. Available to view on YouTube https://www.youtube.com/watch?v=Z3p58Z2zqZo
14. Christopher of Perrevo and Chiliarchos, *History of Suli and Parga*, (Constable, 1823), p. 58.
15. G. Rothenberg, *Napoleon's Great Adversary*, (Spellmount, 1982), p. 76.

Chapter 3

1. G. Rothenberg, *The Military Border in Croatia, 1740-1881*, (Chicago, 1966), p. 87.
2. G. Rothenberg, *The Military Border in Croatia, 1740-1881*, (Chicago, 1966), p. 92.
3. G. Rothenberg, *The Military Border in Croatia, 1740-1881*, (Chicago, 1966), p. 96.
4. M. Hickok, *Ottoman Military Administration in Eighteenth-Century Bosnia*, (Brill, 1997), p. 56.

5   Tax collection, education, legal and religious affairs of non-Muslim communities were administered by their own leaders.
6   The Bogomils were dualists or Gnostics who believed in a world within the body and a world outside the body. They did not use the Christian cross, nor build churches.
7   M. Hickok, *Ottoman Military Administration in Eighteenth-Century Bosnia*, (Brill, 1997), p. 50.
8   Most likely Mustafa Firaki, quoted in E. Hajdarpasic, *Frontier Anxieties*, (Austrian History Yearbook, Volume 51, May 2020), p. 25.
9   K. Sakul, *Ottoman Attempts to Control the Adriatic Frontier in the Napoleonic Wars*, (Proceedings of the British Academy, 156, 2009), p. 255.
10 N. Malcolm, *Rebels, Believers, Survivors: Studies in the History of the Albanians*, (Oxford, 2020), p. 132.
11 R. Carlton and A. Rushworth, *The Krajina Project: Exploring the Ottoman Hapsburg Borderland*, (Proceedings of the British Academy, 156, 2009), p. 412.
12 W. Wittman, *Travels in Turkey, Asia-Minor and Syria*, (Phillips, 1803), p. 57.
13 B. Ozguven, *Palanka Forts and Construction Activity in the Late Ottoman Balkans*, (Proceedings of the British Academy, 156, 2009), p.171.
14 M.Stein, Military Service and Material Gain on the Ottoman Hapsburg Frontier, (Proceedings of the British Academy, 156, 2009), p. 457.
15 P. Brummett, *The Fortress: Defining and Mapping the Ottoman Frontier*, (Proceedings of the British Academy, 156, 2009).
16 R. Carlton and A. Rushworth, *The Krajina Project: Exploring the Ottoman Hapsburg Borderland*, (Proceedings of the British Academy, 156, 2009), p. 418.
17 For a detailed look at the Zadruga, see, J. and B. Halpern, *A Serbian Village in Historical Perspective*, (Irvington, 1984).
18 R. Zens, *Pasvanoglu Osman Pasha and the Pashalik of Belgrade 1791-1807* (International Journal of Turkish Studies, Vol. 8, No. 1, Spring 2002), p. 91.
19 R. Gradeva, *Between Hinterland and Frontier: Ottoman Vidin, Fifteenth to Eighteenth Centuries*, (Proceedings of the British Academy, 156, 2009), p. 340.
20 V. Askan, *Ottoman Wars 1700-1870*, (Pearson, 2007), p. 222.
21 R. Zens, *Pasvanoglu Osman Pasha and the Pashalik of Belgrade 1791-1807* (International Journal of Turkish Studies, Vol. 8, No. 1, Spring 2002), p. 104.
22 N. Malcolm, *Bosnia: A Short History*, (Macmillan, 1996), p. 88.
23 J. Potts, *The Ionian Islands and Epirus*, (Signal Books, 2010), p. 159.
24 W. Plomer, *The Diamond of Jannina*, (Jonathan Cape, 1970), p. 59.
25 Christopher of Perrevo and Chiliarchos, *History of Suli and Parga*, (Constable, 1823), p. 7.
26 Christopher of Perrevo and Chiliarchos, *History of Suli and Parga*, (Constable, 1823), p. 91.
27 Kolokotronis became commander in chief of the Greek forces in Peloponnese in 1825 during the War of Independence..
28 National Archives: FO 78:6, Ambassador in Malta to Foreign Secretary, 12 April 1808.
29 National Archives: FO 78:61 Ali Pasha to Consul, 28 January 1808 (old style).

30. J. Baggally, *Ali Pasha and Great Britain*, (Blackwell, 1938), p. 43.
31. Q and A. Russell, *Ali Pasha, Lion of Ioannina*, (Pen & Sword, 2017), p. 90.
32. National Archives: FO 78:85, Drafts of letters between Lord Castlereagh and Ali Pasha, January 1815.
33. R. Davenport, *The Life of Ali Pasha, Late Vizier of Jannina: Surnamed Aslan, or the Lion*, (London, 1878).
34. W. Plomer, *The Diamond of Jannina*, (Jonathan Cape, 1970), p. 136.
35. E. Said, *Orientalism*, (New York, 1974). K. Fleming, *The Muslim Bonaparte*, (Princeton, 1999) disagrees.
36. N. Malcolm, *Rebels, Believers, Survivors: Studies in the History of the Albanians*, (Oxford, 2020), p. 244.

Chapter 4

1. There was a legal process that gave the captain and crew of Royal Navy ships a share of the value of ships they captured. Frigate captains and crew did particularly well out of this system because they were the main commerce raiders.
2. A. Gosu, *The Third Anti-Napoleonic Coalition and the Sublime Porte*, (International Journal of Turkish Studies 9, No. 1/2), p. 199.
3. For a description of the journey see: V. Bronevskiy, *Northern Tars in Southern Waters*, (Helion, 2019).
4. V. Bronevskiy, *Northern Tars in Southern Waters*, (Helion, 2019), p. 132.
5. N. Saul, *Russia and the Mediterranean 1797-1807*, (University of Chicago, 1970), p. 148.
6. M. Calic, *The Great Cauldron*, (Harvard University Press, 2019), p. 186.
7. M. Broers, *The Napoleonic Mediterranean*, (I. B. Tauris, 2021), p. 10.
8. R. Harris, *Dubrovnik: A History*, (Saqi, 2006), Location 9058.
9. R. Harris, *Dubrovnik: A History*, (Saqi, 2006), Location 9477.
10. N. Saul, *Russia and the Mediterranean 1797-1807*, (University of Chicago, 1970), p. 212.
11. A. Mikaberidze, *Kutuzov: A Life in War and Peace*, (Oxford, 2022), p.281.
12. Writing on 20 August 1795: 'I could, for the asking, get sent to Turkey as general to reorganize the artillery of the Grand Seignior.' R. Johnson, *The Corsican—A Diary of Napoleon's Life in His Own Words*, (Pickle Partners, 2011), Location 211.
13. T. Pocock, *Stopping Napoleon: War and Intrigue in the Mediterranean*, (John Murray, 2004), p. 73.
14. A. Mikhailovsky-Danilevsky, *Russo-Turkish War of 1806-1812*, (Nafziger Collection, 2002), p. 86.
15. Renegade janissary leaders called after the Ottoman Turkish *dayi*, meaning uncle.
16. M. Glenny, *The Balkans 1804-1999*, (Granta, 1999), p. 12.
17. A. Mikhailovsky-Danilevsky, *Russo-Turkish War of 1806-1812*, (Nafziger Collection, 2002), p. 32.
18. T. Pocock, *Stopping Napoleon: War and Intrigue in the Mediterranean*, (John Murray, 2004), p. 99.
19. National Archives: FO 78:61 Constantinople (based at Malta) Embassy reports 1808.

20 W. Laird, *The Royal Navy: a History from the Earliest Times to the Present Day*, (Marston, 1897), p. 423
21 J. Elting, *Swords Around a Throne: Napoleon's Grande Armée*, (The Free Press, 1989), p. 140.

Chapter 5
1 V. Askan, *Ottoman Wars 1700-1870*, (Pearson, 2007), p. 281.
2 F. Ismail, *The Making of the Treaty of Bucharest, 1811-12*, (Middle Eastern Studies Vol. 15, No. 2, May 1979), p. 175.
3 B. Lavery, *Nelson's Navy: Ships, Men, Organisation 1793-1815*, (Conway, 1989), p. 25.
4 P. Mackesy, *The War in the Mediterranean 1803-1810*, (Longmans, 1957), p. 157.
5 For a detailed study of trade issues in the upper Adriatic see: M. Hardy, *The British Navy, Rijeka and A. L. Adamic*, (Archaeopress, 2005).
6 R. Christophe, *Le maréchal Marmont, Duc de Raguse*, (Hachette, 1968), p. 119.
7 Officers like Hoste stretched the rules. See, M. Hardy, *The British and Vis* (Archaeopress, 2009), p. 8.
8 G. Glover, *The Forgotten War Against Napoleon*, (Pen & Sword, 2017), Location 3547.
9 T. Pocock, *Remember Nelson*, (Lume Books, Kindle edition, 2020), p. 159.
10 A. Price, *The Eyes of the Fleet*, (Grafton, 1992), p. 275.
11 W. May, *The Boats of Men of War*, (Caxton, 2003), p. 49.
12 The 44th Foot detachment consisted of ten sergeants, three drummers and 186 men, plus officers. They returned to Sicily in 1810 after being relieved by De Rolle's regiment. T. Carter, *Historical record of the Forty-Fourth or the East Essex Regiment*, (Gale and Polden, 1887), p. 41.
13 A. Nichols, *Wellington's Mongrel Regiment*, (Spellmount, 2005), p. 57.
14 Hudson Lowe became a controversial figure later as Napoleon's jailer in St Helena. Some claim he was responsible for Napoleon's death by his behaviour or even murder.
15 R. Trimen, *An Historical Memoir of the 35th Royal Sussex Regiment of Foot*, (Southampton, 1873), p. 109.
16 National Archives: FO 195:5, Constantinople Embassy, 26 December 1809.
17 M. Feather, *HMS Amphion 1798*, (Feather, 2015), location 583.
18 D. O'Brien, *My Adventures During the Late War*, (Colburn 1839).
19 It was for similar reasons the Allies chose Vis as a commando and partisan base in WW2.
20 The sons of a vineyard owner picked up the game when in Australia, and Lords provided an artificial pitch, equipment and a coach. It is situated next to the WW2 airstrip. This author had the pleasure of bowling on it.
21 J. Henderson, *The Frigates*, (Leo Cooper, 1970), p. 153.
22 M. Hardy, *The British and Vis* (Archaeopress, 2009), covers this debate in detail.
23 M. Hardy, *The British and Vis* (Archaeopress, 2009), p. 84.
24 G. Glover, *Fighting Napoleon*, (Frontline, 2016), p. 77.
25 G. Glover, *The Forgotten War Against Napoleon*, (Pen & Sword, 2017), Location 4313.

26   S, Kneževic and B.Vukićević, *Montenegrin-British Military Cooperation against the French in the Bay of Kotor 1813-1814*, (War in history. Volume 28: Number 4, 2021), p. 792.
27   Anon., *Service Afloat or The Naval Career of Sir William Hoste*, (W. H. Allen, 1887), p. 284.
28   These troops included John Hildebrand, who went on his initiative and describes the siege actions. G. Glover, *Fighting Napoleon*, (Frontline, 2016), Chapters 11-14.
29   Serbian and Montenegrin troops adopted a similar tactic in the Balkan Wars of the 1990's with somewhat less success, although the damage is still visible today.
30   M. Glenny, *The Balkans 1804-1999*, (Granta, 1999), p. 19.

Chapter 6
1   S. Ede-Borrett, *The Army of the Kingdom of Italy 1805-1814*, (Helion, 2022).
2   J. Elting, *Swords Around a Throne: Napoleon's Grande Armée*, (The Free Press, 1989), p. 355.
3   J. Elting, *Swords Around a Throne: Napoleon's Grande Armée*, (The Free Press, 1989), p. 373.
4   National Archives: FO 78:61, Ambassador to Foreign Secretary, 22 April 1808.
5   P. Haythornthwaite, *The Napoleonic Source Book*, (Guild Publishing, 1990), p. 272.
6   For the earlier campaign ORBATs see: R. Goetz, *Russian Land Forces in the Adriatic: 1803-1807*, https://www.napoleon-series.org/military-info/battles/c_ioniansea.html.
7   A. Mikhailovsky-Danilevsky, *Russo-Turkish War of 1806-1812*, (Nafziger Collection, 2002), p. 116.
8   V. Bronevskiy, *Northern Tars in Southern Waters*, (Helion, 2019), p. 90.
9   R. Hopton, *The Battle of Maida 1806*, (Leo Cooper, 2002), p. 73.
10 R. Hopton, *The Battle of Maida 1806*, (Leo Cooper, 2002), p. 85.
11 R. Trimen, *An Historical Memoir of the 35th Royal Sussex Regiment of Foot*, (Southampton, 1873), p. 108.
12 H. Holland, *Travels in the Ionian Islands, Albania, Thessaly, Macedonia during the Years 1812 and 1813*, (Longman, 1815), p. 55.
13 R. Chartrand, *Émigré and Foreign Troops in British Service (2) 1803-1815*, (Osprey, 2000), p. 7.
14 G. Glover, *Fighting Napoleon*, (Frontline, 2016), p. 56.
15 J. Black, *European Warfare 1660-1815*, (UCL Press, 1998), p. 204.
16 S. Shaw, *History of the Ottoman Empire and Modern Turkey, Vol. 1*, (Cambridge, 1976), p. 262.
17 For the detailed organisation: W. Johnson, *The Crescent Among the Eagles*, (Private, 1994), p. 13.
18 C. Flaherty, *The Napoleonic Ottoman Army*, (Partizan Press, 2019).
19 National Archives: FO 95:8:14, State of the Ottoman Navy, 25 April 1787.
20 W. Wittman, *Travels in Turkey, Asia-Minor and Syria*, (Phillips, 1803), p. 63.
21 E. Yener, *Ottoman Seapower and Naval Technology during Catherine II's Turkish Wars 1768-1792* (International Naval Journal, 2016, Vol. 9, Issue 1), p. 9.
22 T. Pocock, *Stopping Napoleon: War and Intrigue in the Mediterranean*, (John Murray, 2004), p. 165.

23 G. Rothenberg, *The Military Border in Croatia, 1740-1881*, (Chicago, 1966), p. 86.
24 P. Haythornthwaite, *Austrian Army of the Napoleonic Wars (2): Cavalry*, (Osprey, 1986). p. 24.
25 D. Hollins, *Austrian Grenadiers and Infantry 1788-1816*, (Osprey, 1998).

ABOUT THE AUTHOR

Dave Watson was born in Liverpool and has been based in Scotland for the last thirty-two years. He lives with his wife Liz and Rasputin (the wargaming cat) in Ayrshire, on the west coast of Scotland.

He is the editor of the website Balkan Military History (www.balkanhistory.org), which has covered the military history of the Balkans for over twenty-three years. He has written for many magazines, journals, and online publications. A list of his publications can be found on the website and his blog, *balkandave.blogspot.com*.

He is the author of *Chasing the Soft Underbelly: Turkey and the Second World War* (Helion, 2023). In addition, he is a contributing author to the books *A New Scotland* (Pluto, 2022), *What Would Keir Hardie Say?* (Luath, 2015), *Keir Hardie and the 21st Century Socialist Revival* (Luath, 2019), and several other current affairs books and publications.

Dave is a graduate in Scots Law from the University of Strathclyde and a Fellow of the Royal Society of Arts. He retired in 2018 from his post as Head of Policy and Public Affairs at UNISON Scotland and now works part-time as a policy consultant.

His passions include wargaming, travel and golf. He is the secretary of Glasgow and District Wargaming Society—one of the UK's longest-running wargame clubs.

You can also follow Dave on Twitter @Balkan_Dave.

www.ingramcontent.com/pod-product-compliance
Lightning Source LLC
Chambersburg PA
CBHW071450080526
44587CB00014B/2061